BANKING ON THE MATURE MARKET

A HANDBOOK
FOR MARKETING
TO THE

50+

CUSTOMER

by
Michael P. Sullivan
Vicki Thomas

Bank Marketing Association
309 W. Washington St.
Chicago, IL 60606

© 1989 Bank Marketing Association
All rights reserved.
Printed in USA.

ISBN 1-55695-000-4

Contents

Preface		iv
Chapter 1	Understanding the Mature Market	1
Chapter 2	Segmenting the Market	18
Chapter 3	Researching the Market	29
Chapter 4	Developing the Package	38
Chapter 5	Examples of Programs that Work	52
Chapter 6	Pre-Retirement Seminars and Social Activities	62
Chapter 7	Communicating with the Mature Market	73
Chapter 8	Tracking Program Results	88
Chapter 9	Staffing	94
Chapter 10	Developing Employee Sensitivity to Mature Customers	106
Conclusion		117
Appendix:	Resources	119
Bibliography		136

Preface

Peter Drucker, the management consultant, is fond of saying that if you are seeking to understand where the world is headed and what is in store for us, study the demographic trends. Anyone who has accepted that philosophy, as we have, can see that the single most dominant socio-economic trend is the aging of the population, not just in the United States but in the industrialized and undeveloped nations of the world.

We believe the demographic trend in aging will have enormous impact on the retail bank of the future. Already, some leaders in the financial services community have understood what is happening and are pushing their institutions into developing programs that provide a toehold in the seniors market and a giant step into the future. One major regional bank chief executive we know has made a strategic decision to focus on the bank's ability to serve this burgeoning marketplace with better services, better communications and better employee understanding of mature customers.

We have watched developments in the financial services industry carefully, and we are seeing the light go on in the executive suites of many banks. Bankers, even those outside the geographic areas where older people retire such as the Sun Belt, are beginning to understand that their business is subject to change—right underneath them. The credit-hungry young professional, the young family with its needs and the family struggling to provide a college education for its children are those from whom most retail-oriented banks make their money.

Partially hidden, and sometimes ignored, is the 50-plus aged customers—the mature market. Unless they are candidates for private banking or trust services, they have largely been overlooked by banking in general.

Now, the numbers are starting to be known—65 to 80 percent of a typical bank's savings deposits are held by a small number of customers—under 20 percent. And, banks are beginning to recognize their impact, and are beginning to ask, "How can we guarantee their loyalty?"

The most important part of this question is that it is starting to be asked. And, bankers are finding out that the answer is not as simple as they might think. The bank should not apply standards used with the younger customer to the older bank customer. These individuals are different. They think differently and act differently. They have values different from others.

This handbook is developed as a desk-top reference source for bankers seeking to enhance their programs, as well as those who want to know how to start a seniors program. We believe the chapters capture the essence of any seniors program. They are as follows:

Chapter 1 Understanding the Market
Chapter 2 Segmenting the Market
Chapter 3 Researching the Market
Chapter 4 Developing the Package
Chapter 5 Examples of Programs that Work
Chapter 6 Pre-Retirement Seminars and Social Activities
Chapter 7 Communicating with the Market
Chapter 8 Tracking the Results
Chapter 9 Staffing
Chapter 10 Developing Employee Sensitivity

Because there are a number of myths and stereotypes about the mature market, we decided to address them in each chapter. The reader will note that each chapter begins with a list of common mistakes marketers make in dealing with the mature market. We address most of those common mistakes in the chapter. At the conclusion of the chapter, we include a list of recommendations in each subject area.

While "mature" may be defined differently by banks, we have chosen age 50 as the starting point for the mature market. This is already a common definition for many banks. We feel 50 provides a larger market potential and that age 50 is perceived to be a transition point in life—a time when individuals begin to focus more on rewarding themselves and finding life more satisfying.

A final thought—in writing this handbook, we were made much more aware of the need on the part of bank marketers to obtain the ongoing commitment of executive management. The need is vital for the marketer to have adequate promotional dollars, a staff to run the programs and a reasonable budget to make it appear the bank is doing everything it can for this important customer base. We are convinced that the mature market will be a major strategic battleground in the financial services industry for the rest of this century.

Acknowledgements

Many people contributed to this handbook in various ways. It is the result of information collected from telephone interviews and visits with banks that have senior programs and suppliers who provide consulting and packaged programs in the mature market area.

We gratefully acknowledge bank personnel and outside suppliers that shared invaluable information with us on the mature market. Without their input this project would not have been possible.

We personally thank BMA staff for their input, guidance and interest in the mature market.

One final note of appreciation goes to our families, who enabled us to have time away to write this handbook.

July 1, 1989

Vicki Thomas   Michael P. Sullivan

1 Understanding the Mature Market

Common Mistakes

1 Continuing to pursue a retail banking strategy emphasizing the 25 to 49 age group exclusively and missing the opportunity to capture high balance accounts held by seniors.

2 Failure to understand the relationship between an aging America and the impact on the bank's customer base, as the older customer controls the vast majority of savings deposits.

3 Lack of appreciation of the aging baby boomer trend and the development of future banking services, as the boomers in 1996 begin to move into the ranks of older Americans.

4 Developing mature market programs based on the banker's personal feelings, often mistaken, about the market without further analysis or verification.

5 Using chronological age as the primary criterion for making strategic decisions about the seniors market.

One of the early disciples of seniors marketing is Ken Dychtwald. In his recent book, *Age Wave: The Challenges and Opportunities of an Aging America,* he says, "I became increasingly excited about what I saw as a really big story: the absolutely predictable arrival, in our culture and in our time, of a demographic revolution that has no precedent in history. The very thing that we had blanked out of our cultural life was about to overwhelm us. Our young country is growing old. But are we prepared? The answer is no—at least, not yet."

Whether or not our banks are prepared, the mature market offers an unusual and remarkable opportunity for retail banking organizations to develop a special relationship with a highly important and profitable segment. Some banks have caught on to what the opportunity represents. Others have looked at it and made the judgment that older customers should not be treated any differently from any others. Still other bankers have not explored the potential in any meaningful way.

Whatever choice is made, it is clear that competition for the financial accounts of mature customers is increasing. From what we have seen across the country, we believe the mature market will become a major strategic battleground between financial services of all kinds. Take for example the American Association of Retired Persons (AARP). The organization represents close to 30 million members over 50 years of age. It is in a variety of businesses—health insurance, magazine publishing, auto and home insurance, travel service, mutual funds, pharmaceutical services and motor club services.

AARP has formed a federal credit union, even though it was already providing investment, insurance and travel services for its members. It plans to build a nationwide financial service offering credit cards, share accounts, certificates of deposits, use of ATMs and debit cards. If the AARP credit union nets as little as three percent of its existing 30 million AARP members, it will become the largest credit union in existence.

The AARP and others—like the insurance-dominant USAA in San Antonio, Texas, with a membership of 1,700,000 military retirees and their families—are major nationwide providers in a position to provide financial services to the mature customer. So are Merrill Lynch, American Express, Sears and a host of other nationwide financial providers. In local markets, the strongest competition is likely to come from commercial banks and savings and loans. We estimate that about 1,500 banks in the U.S. have seniors clubs or seniors accounts already. The number will increase sharply in the near term.

Dychtwald and others, as we shall see later, believe marketers from many types of businesses do not fully understand the value of the mature market and have not set about to find ways to differentiate their business to appeal to the seniors market.

One thing is certain. The facts about the growing "mature market" are most impressive. Predictions are that within 10 years the market will replace the "yuppies" as the most important demographic market for most consumer businesses. A report published by the U.S. Senate Special Committee on Aging provides an overview of key health, income, employment, housing and social statistics of today's older population. Among the highlights of the report are:[1]

- The number of persons age 65 and over is growing more rapidly than the rest of the U.S. population.

- In 1900, one in 10 Americans was age 55 and over and one in 25 was age 65 and older. By 1986, one in five was 55 years and older and one in eight was 65 years and older.

- The older population grew more than twice as fast as the rest of the population during the last decade. Today there are as many Americans aged 55 and over as there are teenagers.

- The median age of the U.S. population is projected to rise from age 31.8 today to age 36 by the year 2000 and to age 42 by the year 2040.

The Size of the Mature Market

The actual size of the mature market may be analyzed by reviewing a series of tables. Table 1—Distribution of the Population by Age Groups provides an overall look at the age brackets of seniors.

Table 1—Distribution of the Population by Age Groups: 1986

Age Groups	Number (in Thousands)	Percent
All ages	241,596	100
0 to 54	190,193	79
55 to 64	22,230	9
65 to 74	17,325	7
75 to 84	9,051	4
85-plus	2,796	1
55-plus	51,403	21
65-plus	29,173	12

Source: U.S. Bureau of the Census, "Estimates of the Population of the United States, by Age, Sex, and Race: 1980-1986." Current Population Reports Series P-25, No. 1000 (February, 1987). Note that the age brackets do not coincide with our preference—age 50 and up.

Analyzing the distribution of the older population in its current form tells only part of the story for the banking organization intent on developing strategies directed to the mature market. More important, an appreciation of what's ahead for those who are considering long-term strategies is available from studying data contained in Table 2—Elderly Population: 1980-2040.

Table 2—Elderly Population: 1980-2040

	65 Years and Older	75 Years and Older (Number in Millions)	85 Years and Older
1980	25.7	10.1	2.3
1990	31.8	13.7	3.5
2000	35.0	17.3	5.1
2010	39.3	19.0	6.8
2020	51.4	21.6	7.3
2030	64.3	29.9	8.8
2040	66.6	37.5	12.9

Source: U.S. Census Bureau Current Population Series P-23, No. 138, "Demographic and Socioeconomic Aspects of Aging in the United States," 1984.

This table contains projections of the population levels of the mature market for the next 50 years in which all age brackets will have sizable increases. The maps on the following pages show the distribution and growth of the over-65 population in the U.S.

The United States is at a significant turning point sociologically, culturally and economically. These older Americans are living longer and remaining in much better health than their predecessors. This segment is not only growing rapidly, but it has imposing financial numbers. It is a target group deserving priority consideration by every consumer banking organization, even if a bank does so as a defensive posture.

"Older Americans will be a huge market for businesses that can help them save and manage money," says Jeff Ostroff, vice president and

3

partner of the PrimeLife Marketing Division of the Data Group, Inc., in Plymouth Meeting, Pennsylvania.[2] "The 41 million prime lifers, aged 50 to 64, will offer the greatest business potential. The prime lifers of tomorrow know they need to plan for a retirement that could last over 30 years. And many do not believe they can depend on Social Security or Medicare."

The Banking Opportunity

For banking institutions specifically, the mature market represents:[3]

- Higher than average bank deposit levels and banking relationships. In fact, according to the American Bankers Association, customers over 50 years of age account for a minimum of 60 percent of commercial banking deposits nationwide. The U.S. League of Savings Institutions says that more than 80 percent of thrift deposits are held by those over age 50.

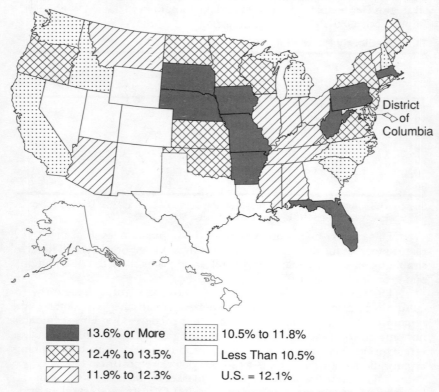

Persons 65+ As Percentage of Total Population: 1986

- 13.6% or More
- 12.4% to 13.5%
- 11.9% to 12.3%
- 10.5% to 11.8%
- Less Than 10.5%
- U.S. = 12.1%

SOURCE: U.S. Bureau of the Census. "State Population and Household Estimates with Age, Sex, and Components of Change: 1981 to 1986." *Current Population Reports* Series P-25, No. 1010 (September 1987).

- An average savings account balance of $3,000, not including certificates of deposit. For banking services and seniors clubs and accounts, the average is closer to $21,000.
- Higher checking account balances. Accounts held by customers over 50 years of age average $3,000 more than other age groups.
- Total financial relationships. This age group owns nearly half of all corporate stocks and holds two-thirds of all portfolios of $25,000 or more. Nearly 75 percent of households represented by this group own their own homes and 80 percent of those homes are mortgage-free.
- Financial control. Seniors control more than 75 percent of the nation's wealth and account for 42 percent of all after-tax household income. This is the equivalent of $160 billion in discretionary income—representing one-half of the U.S. total.

Percent Increase in Population 65+: 1980-86

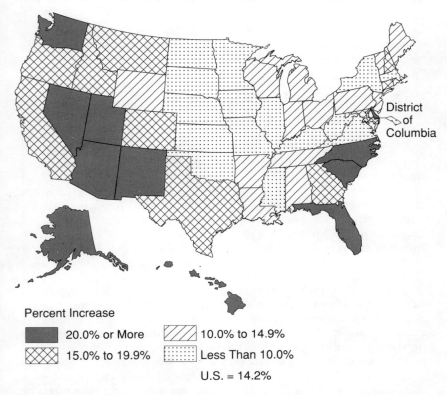

Percent Increase
- 20.0% or More
- 15.0% to 19.9%
- 10.0% to 14.9%
- Less Than 10.0%

U.S. = 14.2%

SOURCE: U.S. Bureau of the Census. "State Population and Household Estimates with Age, Sex, and Components of Change: 1981 to 1986." *Current Population Reports* Series P-25, No. 1010 (September 1987).

Banks are responding to this market potential and appealing to it in a number of innovative ways, hoping to catch the fancy of older customers.

- SouthTrust Bank of Alabama, Birmingham, developed the ID CD that pays a bonus rate based on the age of the purchaser. The eight-month certificate requires a $500 minimum deposit. At the time of purchase, the customer receives a bonus of one basis point for each year of age.

- Westborough Savings Bank in Westborough, Massachusetts, and Rio Salado Bank in Tempe, Arizona, have a similar approach. They have established bank branches in retirement villages for residents of seniors high rise apartments, nursing homes, and other elderly living quarters.[4]

- Chemical Bank, New York City, is offering free advice for the affluent self-employed professionals, corporate directors and small business owners. Retirement planning, says a bank spokesman, remains one of the few hefty tax deductions for the self-employed.[5]

- After security regulatory approval, Southern Federal Savings, Atlanta, put three mobile branches on the road serving 20 nursing homes.[6]

The Financial Condition of the Mature Customer

By all benchmarks—financial assets, net worth, and income flow—today's consumers aged 60 and over are much better off than their predecessors, according to Sandra van der Merwe, Professor of International Marketing and Services at the International Institute, Geneva, Switzerland.[7]

Purchasing Power—When they were in their 30s, 40s and early 50s, during the prosperous decades of the 1950s, 60s and 70s, many were able both to accumulate assets and benefit more from freely available employer pension plans. As a plus, Social Security has been indexed to inflation and real estate values have soared. The result is that the retired middle class now is able to maintain its purchasing power later in life than previously had been the case.

The retired middle class, more than any segment of the population, has benefitted from the prosperous post-World War II economy. The market is a broad one with many segments: at one end is the middle-aged market, which may start as young as 45, and at the other end are retirees aged 65 and up. Many now find themselves with plump pensions and with homes, savings and investments that have appreciated handsomely.[8]

Incomes—In the last decade the income of the 60-and-older consumer has increased by almost 10 percent annually, faster than any other age group. These well-off seniors have more per capita income

6

today than those under 45. Projections for the next 15 years are that real household incomes will go up by 40 percent, raising living standards even further.[9]

The financial independence of the older person is a fact of life and one which financial services marketers need to be aware of. One way to look at this independence is the fact that in the mid-1940s, 40 percent of older parents received most of their financial support from their children. Because of the impact of Social Security and other factors, today the amount is around one percent. In today's situation, older parents are twice as likely to give their children money as to receive it from them.

Health—Contrary to the stereotype, most older persons view their health positively. Although most older people have at least one chronic condition, seven out of 10 elderly who are not hospitalized describe their health as good or excellent compared to others their age.

The over-60 consumer is healthier, more mobile, more enthusiastic and more flexible than in previous times. According to a report published by the U.S. Senate Committee on Aging, chronic ailments have decreased. Seniors are generally in better shape because of better care and facilities, increased health awareness and medical breakthroughs. The majority of Americans follow some sort of exercise routine and statistics show that phsyical activity, even at a fairly advanced age, has a rejuvenating effect.

Interests—The seniors market is diverse. It is interested in a variety of subjects, a fact that is not well understood by marketers. Following is a listing of major activities and experiences in which seniors with incomes of $30,000 have a relatively high index when compared with adults of all ages. (An index of 137 means that the activity is 37 percent more apt to occur than with the base group of adults of all ages.)

Activity	Index
Own a vacation/weekend home	237
Bought travelers checks in the last 12 months with a total value of $1,000-1,999	204
Belong to Reader's Digest Book Club	189
Have a long-term savings certificate at a bank or savings and loan	175
Ordered vitamins by mail in last 12 months	171
Own a new car, domestic luxury class	169
Own an electric mixer	160
Own an electric yard grass trimmer	147
Traveled on a scheduled/chartered flight for a domestic vacation	141
Own an outboard motor under 25 horsepower	129

Source: Private Eye Target, Simmons Market Research, 1987

While these statistics represent the upscale side of the mature market, it is clear there is opportunity for financial services marketers. These discerning adult consumers have the uncommitted dollars that allow them to select the more luxurious version of many products and services. For marketers, this means understanding that they want box seats, not bleacher seats, luxury cars, not economical ones, wool and silk instead of polyester. They can afford to choose name brands over generic brands or private labels, and they opt for Perrier instead of city water.

The Long-Term Outlook for the Mature Market: Stable

Today, dramatic changes are underway. A study, "The Mature Americans,"[10] by the Daniel Yankelovich Group states:

> The changes are rooted in demographics; baby boomers are older, the birth rate has declined and medical technology has raised life expectancies, which have all contributed to a rise in the nation's median age. Like the period of the 1960s, demographic changes have been accompanied by value shifts, with equally profound implications. Today's mature Americans have altered many of their own assumptions and life goals. They can no longer be ignored because they are committed to living life to the fullest.

The Yankelovich study also revealed three major findings in its investigation of values, attitudes, lifestyles and behaviors of people over 50 and the subsequent generation of 39-to-49-year-olds.

1. *Men and women 50 years and older are a highly attractive group for marketers.* They exhibit a strong commitment to spending on products and services that enhance their personal enjoyment of life. Now that financial and family obligations have been met, they have a greater sense of accomplishment. In short, they now feel entitled to a certain amount of self-indulgence and have the income to act.
2. *The projected profile of the 50-plus population should remain stable for the next five to 10 years.* The most striking finding of the study was the remarkable consistency between values, attitudes and consumer orientations of the 39-49 generation and its over-50 counterparts. According to the study, this is a reflection of the diminishing values gap among all age groups in society. The 39-to-49-year-old does not differ markedly from the current 50-plus person. This enables marketers to plan strategies, introduce new products and develop communications for those over 50 today wthout concern that those strategies will become obsolete in a few years due to the generation gap.
3. *Differences are evident between people 39-49 and those over 50, mostly in their behavior.* Although the two groups display great similarities in attitudes, there are expectedly some behavioral differences between them. Most of these differences are related to physical aging and are manifested by such adjustments as more home-centered activities and fewer active sports.

Over-50 consumers are more involved in socially responsible activities, such as community and church-related work. This humanitarianism is a sentiment shared widely among Americans over 50 and coexists with a need for personally fulfilling experiences.

The aggressive, affluent older consumers do not hoard their money in mattresses as their parents and grandparents might have done. Today they reward themselves by spending more now that they have moved through the life cycle and their financial obligations have lessened. According to a recent Gallup Study, the mature consumer is inclined to look beyond the price tag to buy based on the quality of the product and upon the friendliness of the service.

The Difference Between Older and Younger Consumers

Understanding the buying behavior of sectors of the mature market is extremely valuable in understanding what motivates the older customers. A perspective of the differences between older and younger consumers is provided by David Wolfe:[11]

Consumers buy products and services because they need them, they desire them or both. Purchases based on need alone are nondiscretionary. In general, consumers find satisfaction in life by fulfilling their desires, rather than their needs.

Younger people get satisfaction by owning products such as cars, stereos and homes. The "possession experience" is a strong focus in the lives of younger people, especially the first time they buy something, i.e., the first car or the first home. As they grow older, many people shift their focus toward services or "catered experiences." Travel, restaurants, art, and major sports events assume a larger role in the quest for satisfaction. An older person is likely to hire someone to take care of mundane chores, such as mowing the lawn or painting the house.

Those who spend most of their discretionary dollars on possessions tend to be aged 40 or younger. Those who spend most on catered experiences tend to be aged 40 to 60. Among those aged 60 to 80, discretionary purchases are influenced by "being experiences." These include interpersonal relationships, philosophical introspection, and the conscious seeking out and contemplation of the joys of living. Product- and service-generated feelings provide less satisfaction as intangible things grow in importance, like getting in touch with one's self, enjoying a sunset, taking a walk in the woods, or having a friendly conversation.

Appealing to Life Satisfaction

Because the primary goal of a market-driven organization is to provide improved satisfaction to markets which have been targeted for attention, marketers attempt to gain competitive advantage through dealing with those perceived needs and wants. The added dimension of "life satisfaction" provides marketers with a unique opportunity to create a differential advantage.

Life satisfaction reflects one's ability to take pleasure in everyday activities, to consider life meaningful, to hold an optimistic outlook, to feel successful in achieving goals, and to hold a positive sense of one's self.

Having enough money to lessen the fear and concern over living an additional 20 to 30 years after retiring from work is of paramount importance to those nearing retirement and those who have retired. Money is frequently mentioned as the key to a happy retirement, but Rutgers University psychologist Daniel Ogilvie has found another, much more important factor.[12]

According to Ogilvie, once an individual has an adequate amount of money, life satisfaction depends for the most part on how much time the older person spends doing meaningful things. He believes retirement-planning workshops and seminars should spend more time helping people decide how to use their skills and interests after they retire.

Looking at the attitudes of the older person is helpful in understanding the older consumer. So, too, is understanding how the older consumer makes decisions, and why it is important for the bank to build relationships through social events like wine and cheese receptions, group tours and trips, seminars on financial planning and group health events like walkers' rallies or seniors games. There are those who believe that discounts and free banking services are far less important to seniors than the social aspects of events and other bank-sponsored activities.

Buying Behavior of Older Consumers

Banks need to consider certain significant buying characteristics of the market:

Mature consumers do more shopping. They tend to shop earlier in the day. They do more store shopping, looking for the right products. They are experienced shoppers, many with 30 to 40 years of shopping experience. Bank marketers must expect the mature customer to shop for value in financial product offerings, compare offerings from one bank to another and make decisions after shopping extensively.

The elderly have a perspective on convenience different from that of younger people. They are not concerned with the time it takes but the effort required to shop. Retirees in particular have a fair amount of time to do things, so they are able to take the time to research purchase options.

Convenience is an issue that many bank marketers rightly believe is crucial to their bank's strategy. But marketers are also coming to understand that "convenience" may be interpreted as locational convenience, product convenience, service convenience and even market segment convenience.

A problem for bank marketers is superimposing their own beliefs on a market segment with the result that they "mismarket." A recent example is shown in the results of a study by the Daniel Yankelovich Group. Microwave ovens, video cassette recorders, automatic teller machines and other consumer devices are marketed as time savers, but the companies and advertising agencies selling them may be missing out on a much larger market opportunity.

The study concluded that older Americans, whom marketers have viewed typically as resistant to new technology, in fact reject many products because they are advertised as time-saving conveniences. Only a third of Americans in their 60s and fewer in their 70s say they are "always looking for new ways to save time," the survey reported. Instead, those who are retired often have little but time, so they tend to look for activities, such as cooking, that take up time.[13]

"The market isn't attuned to the needs of older people," said Daniel Yankelovich, chairman of the firm that did the research. He cited automatic teller machines as a technology designed for convenience and time saving, whereas older Americans are looking for something that's time-filling.

Focus group research conducted as part of the study shows that the older person prefers dealing with a teller rather than dealing with an ATM. The objective for bank marketers may be to redesign ATMs to include other functions that would make them more appealing to the mature market. This means that the ATM's appeal of time convenience, which is extremely attractive to the younger customer, is not necessarily appealing to the older customer.

Older people are more interested in value. They look for price promotions, cents-off, discounts, reduced rates, rebates, end-of-season sales, special promotions and bargain basement sales. As one senior said in a focus group session, "We are coupon fiends." And, as pointed out earlier, they have the time to do the shopping required to find the values. For the bank marketer, the appeal of free checking, discounted financial services and lower rate loans and higher rate savings and investments has appeal to the mature market.

Seniors are more interested in product information and are less responsive to lifestyle advertising. The mature customer reads more than the younger market. They are particularly receptive to rational explanations of the products. For the financial services marketer, this means copy should have rational appeal. We know of one major seniors program in which the bank will only allow the president of the agency to write its seniors promotions because of his ability to write copy with rational appeal.

Older consumers tend to be aggressive consumers. They are serious "consumerologists," as Florence Skelly, of the Daniel Yankelovich Group, calls them. As a matter of routine, older consumers tend to make decisions based on price comparisons. They pride themselves on being good shoppers. They are open to price promotions. Bank marketers need to take the older customer and mature market seriously and understand their penchant for shopping.

Ask "How Old Do You Feel?" and Study the Answer

An important lesson for marketers is that chronological age is not a valid differentiator of the older adult market. The mature market thinks of itself in cognitive, not chronological, terms. When asked "How old do you feel?," older people normally indicate that they feel as many as 10 years younger than their age. For example, 70-year-olds will say they feel more like 60 years of age. This is a significant fact for financial service marketers.

Frequently, bank marketers have identified the market in terms of age-only segmenting. However, with this market, one measure such as age turns out to be a poor or inexact method of defining the market. And, more important, it does not aid the marketer in understanding the many hidden motivational factors in the mature consumer's make-up.

The Key "Life Event" for Those Over 50—Retirement

Retirement is the key event in the lives of those over 50 years of age, and there is much thought and consternation over it. The most pressing need of seven in 10 people interviewed for a "Retired in America" study by the Retirement Advisors Division of Hearst Business Publication was for retirement planning information.

The Hearst study was done twice, in 1984 and 1988. There are a number of surprises in the responses in the intervening years: An increase in the average household income; a decrease in the number of retirees moving to another state; an increase in the number of retirees who did not want to work in retirement and an increase in the use of senior citizen activities. The survey revealed a fair amount of independence on the part of most retirees. Both years, about 94 percent of the respondents said they did not receive any physical assistance from relatives and 98 percent said they did not receive any financial help whatsoever. The results contradict the belief of many that the elderly are physically and financially dependent on their family for support.

Are retirees anxious to get back into the labor force? More than 70 percent of respondents said they were not interested in work at all. Asked if they looked for employment during the past year, 95 percent said they had not.

One other important clue about this group and their financial solvency may be apparent in the statistics about housing. Nearly 85 percent of them own their own homes and 82 percent have paid off their mortgages. In both surveys, most people did not move, contrary to what one might expect of recently retireds. Of those who did, 18 percent moved to a new state, 11 percent moved to a new town in the same state and eight percent moved to another house in the same town.

As far as their health goes, 67 percent reported their health as good or excellent and 58 percent reported no change in health since retirement. Although 65 percent reported they had not developed any new leisure or educational interests in retirement, almost 44 percent resumed an interest or activity limited to them during their work years. Fishing, golf and reading were the top three activities.

In the latest survey, 68 percent said they had no formal retirement preparation. Those who did have some training, said they did it on their own. One conclusion is that there is a lack of effort on the part of a diverse group—management, labor and academia—to provide these tools to make their retirement more rewarding.

In this century, retirement has become an expected part of an individual's life course. In 1900, the average male spent three percent of his life in retirement. In 1980, he was spending nearly one-fifth or 13.8 years of his life in retirement. And, while age 65 is commonly thought of as the "normal" retirement age, almost two-thirds of older workers retire before age 65.

As the senior market segment becomes larger, more people in it retire. And, with retirement comes more freedom and free time that make seniors unique among market segments.[14] Voluntary retirement is becoming popular in America, and not because of poor health. Research in 1982 reveals that more than half of those who retire do so because they want to and look forward to it.[15] With more time on their hands and the motivation to go with it, older consumers are more active and versatile than ever before.

Average retirement age is just over 60—a sign that many are making a commitment to retirement at an earlier age than the commonly accepted age 65. The vast majority of those 60 and over now lead independent lives and aggressively pursue new and more exciting lifestyles. With educational levels going up across the globe, these consumers start out with a wider perspective, knowledge of their options and a higher level of discernment and sophistication. They also have a broader range of interests and creative activities.

In short, their lifestyles and consumption patterns are more adventuresome than those of their ancestors. And experts predict that as the baby boomers move into this phase they will bring with them their vigorous spending patterns and boost this market's potential even more.[16]

One consideration for those facing retirement in addition to their financial needs is where they will live. Where do they spend their retirement years? While many pre-retirees and retirees talk about their dreams to relocate to tropical paradises or sun-drenched climates, and many have the wherewithal to do so, few do. Most people remain in the same county they have always lived in. According to the U.S. Census Bureau, only three percent of those age 55 and over relocate to another state. As a result, more than half of the mature adults reside in the following states, listed by population size:

1. California
2. New York
3. Florida
4. Pennsylvania
5. Texas
6. Illinois
7. Ohio
8. Michigan

As the more mobile, "baby boomer" population ages, individuals and families are more likely to relocate to another state. They are already accustomed to living away from the extended family and are likely to find relocation to be part of their overall retirement plans. This factor will place new demands on the housing industry as this group searches for luxury care living complete with exercise rooms, saunas, swimming pools and golf courses.

An Important Differentiator—Level of Service

One of the most important areas in bank marketing today is customer satisfaction with banking services. What does the mature market want in terms of banking services? Bankers think their definition of quality service is the same as older customer's. As it turns out, customer service definitions vary widely by customer groups. One person with first-hand knowledge of customer perception of service quality is Bill Angell, president, Angell & Company, Westport, Connecticut, and a long-time bank advertising researcher. His comments provide insight for advertising campaigns, themes or copy approaches directed to the seniors market.

Based on client research and his company's annual "Quality of Services" interviews with 400,000 bank customers over the years, Angell says that older customers are more satisfied with the services they receive from banks than are younger customers.[17]

There are similarities and there are differences—not always predictable. The most important service issue to both older and younger customers is that the bank have well-trained tellers and equally well-trained officers.

Other areas where they differ:

- Easy to understand statements. This is a relatively unimportant issue to younger customers but an extremely important one to older customers.

- Being responsive to inquiries. This is very important to younger customers and not all that important to older customers.

■ Trying hard to please. It is very important to older customers that bank employees appear to try hard to solve problems on their behalf.

What other service factors rank high with the older adult? They want the bank to be free of bookkeeping errors; have the ability to correct errors quickly; have courteous and friendly tellers and equally courteous and friendly officers.

What factors are not important to older customers, according to his survey? Personnel who know their name, employees who know loan rates, the bank having automatic teller machines, waiting in teller lines and high interest rates on certificates of deposits. A number of these factors are contrary to what banks think is important to their older customers.

Any surprises in his findings? Only that there dramatic differences in responses by sex. "Women are far more demanding, expect much more from their financial institution and are more critical than senior men," said Angell. "This is so on almost every issue: responsiveness, training, friendliness, any of the major issues."

According to Angell, the market is not what it seems to be and marketers need to look more closely at what the segment considers important.

The Failure of Many Marketers to Understand

Yet even with these facts presented by demographers and researchers in studies of the 50-plus age groups, marketers have been slow to develop programs and services targeted to what has turned out to be a robust population segment.

There is the belief among marketers that this segment possesses limited economic potential, but this is mistaken. The work of demographers, gerontologists, economists and market researchers does not support such a hypothesis. People over age 50 are emerging as one of the largest and most powerful market segments in our country today. Until recently, this market has been largely ignored.

Marketers of any consumer product or service are going to have to take off the blinders about the mature market. It is becoming critical that all must rethink their programs, product lines and approaches or find themselves out of touch with the marketplace realities.

Another critic of today's marketing practices is Fabian Linden, Director of the Consumer Research Center, The Conference Board.[18]

To the marketing and advertising fraternities, those who are no longer young are a forgotten generation. We are clearly a youth-oriented culture. The perception of the young is one of promise, glamour—those who are receptive to new ideas, new products. Those who are no longer young are considered dowdy, uninspired and, if not entirely dismissed by marketers, certainly largely neglected. In some vague way they are conceived as a segment of the market that offers little excitement or opportunity.

15

While the seniors market is a relatively new phenomenon, it offers huge profit potential, says Jim Schneider, president, the Jim Schneider Group, Oak Brook, Illinois.[19]

It's time to look it over closely. You can target this segment using sophisticated research information that has been developed on lifecycles and psychographic profiles, as well as by honing your own instincts for selling. Unfortunately, few bank marketing professionals are using what they know about seniors to sell them more products. What good is free checking for seniors or costly seniors clubs and special marketing programs if they aren't means of increasing business from key accounts, or if branch salespeople sell single products instead of relationships?

Most bank marketing executives fall into one of two groups: researchers who know seniors but don't know selling, and people who know selling but don't know seniors. It's time the twain should meet because the new seniors are a vibrant marketing niche.

In our minds, the mature market is more complex than it looks. It will grow more complex as competitors develop marketing strategies that are innovative and powerful. The mature market is one that bankers, marketers and others need to keep on top of.

Our Recommendations

☐ Analyze the demographics in the bank's trading area as they relate to the post-50 market. Use a technique combining geography and demographics. Through zip-code analysis, identify pockets of seniors by zip code down to the tract level.

☐ Review the bank's retail customer profile to determine type and size of customer by account or account relationships by age and income levels.

☐ Using breakpoints at ages 40, 45, 50, 55, 60, 65, 70, 75 and 80, determine the age distribution of your bank customers. Consider the development of a strategy involving retail banking, trust banking and private banking.

☐ Monitor the activity of competitive financial services in the mature market. Shop competitor locations to obtain information about their seniors account or club.

☐ Survey the branch staff on the older customer—their perception of the numbers, the banking habits of seniors, the services seniors are interested in, what competitors are offering to seniors. Determine which branches have the most seniors for specialized attention.

☐ Visit community social services, health agencies, senior centers, seniors condominiums and apartment buildings, and religious groups providing assistance to the elderly to determine potential tie-ins and resources for the bank's program.

☐ Assemble a seniors advisory board on an informal or formal basis to help determine potential in the market and begin to prepare for the eventuality of offering specialized services.

☐ For banks with an existing program much of the same might apply if the objective is to develop enhancements to the current program.

Notes

1. "Aging America: Trends and Projections," 1987-88 Edition, U.S. Senate Special Committee on Aging in conjunction with the American Association of Retired Persons, the Federal Council on the Aging and the U.S. Administration on Aging.
2. Jeff Ostroff, "An Aging Market: How Business Can Prosper," *American Demographics,* May, 1989, P. 26.
3. *The Statistical Handbook on Aging Americans,* Oryx Press. Statistics used in this section came from a number of tables in the book.
4. Jay Rosenstein, "Bank Branches in Retirement Villages Tap Lucrative Market With Small Outlay," *American Banker,* July 28, 1988, P. 1.
5. "Chem's Pitching Pensions to Well-To-Do Self-Employed," *Crain's New York Business,* January 16, 1989, P. 22.
6. "Going for the Gray," *ABA Banking Journal,* April, 1989, P. 43.
7. Sandra van der Merwe, "GRAMPIES: A New Breed of Consumers Comes of Age," *Business Horizons,* November-December, 1987, P. 14.
8. Hilary Stout, "Free at Last—To Spend More Money," *New York Times,* September 11, 1988.
9. *Chartbook on Aging,* P. 136.
10. Study released in fall, 1987, for the American Association of Retired Persons magazine, *Modern Maturity.*
11. David Wolfe, "The Ageless Market," *American Demographics,* July, 1987, P. 2.
12. "The 'Gray Boom' in Marketing," Op. Cit., P. 49.
13. Randall Rothenberg, "Campaigns That Turn Off Older Americans," *New York Times,* May 30, 1988.
14. "GRAMPIES: A New Breed of Consumers Comes of Age," Op. Cit., P. 14.
15. S. Sherman, "Reported Reason Retired Workers Left Their Last Job: Findings From the New Beneficiary Survey," *Social Security Bulletin,* March 1987, P. 25.
16. "GRAMPIES: A New Breed of Consumers Comes of Age," P. 14.
17. Telephone interview with Bill Angell by Michael P. Sullivan, January 16, 1989.
18. The Conference Board, "Midlife and Beyond: The $800 Billion Over-Fifty Market," 1985, Prepared by the Consumer Research Center in a study sponsored by CBS/Broadcast Group, CBS Magazine and CBS Economics.
19. Jim Schneider, "Seniors—The Rising Stars of Relationship Banking," *Bank Marketing,* January, 1987, P. 42.

2 Segmenting the Market

Common Mistakes

1 Placing all bank customers 50 and over into one general category and and using one message for all.

2 Not understanding the different financial product and service needs of the various mature market sub-groups.

3 Taking older customers for granted by assuming they will remain loyal to the bank, because they tend to resist changing banking relationships.

4 Assuming that one general advertising and promotional campaign aimed at all customers 50 and older will maintain active, lasting bank relationships.

5 Developing a program designed for customers 50 and over without conducting adequate market research to understand the different attitudes, financial product needs, and influences of the various mature market sub-groups.

6 Not pre-testing promotional campaigns targeted to customers 50 and over to find out if there is anything negative to this market segment in the message.

7 Maintaining that a free checking account with a minimum balance of $100 entitling customers to certain privileges and services is enough to command their loyalty and continued customer use.

A pproximately 1,500 banks offer special programs and services targeted to the 50 and over customer. In our telephone interview surveys of selected banks, less than one percent indicated they were segmenting 50-plus bank customers into various sub-groups. And, in fact, most surveyed felt the process was too time consuming, and said most people 50 and over were generally alike.

The truth of the matter is that the mature market is not homogeneous. Lumping together all bank customers 50 and over is a major mistake that is being made by most in the financial sector. One cannot assume that an active, still-employed 50-year-old has the same financial product and service needs as that of a 70-year-old active, retired, individual. The needs are different, not only financially but emotionally.

Younger members of the mature market tend to be more self-sufficient, still married, with a close-knit circle of friends to support them. Marketing strategies currently used by banks tend to be most effective with this group. Bank customers in the older groups are perceived to be firmly entrenched in their current banking relationships, and consequently those relationships have become less important to the bank.

Segmenting the Mature Market

Why is it important to segment the mature customer base into various groups? As more and more financial institutions begin to market more aggressively to older consumers, they will be inundated with offers of special membership privileges that will begin to sound the same. Differentiating financial services benefits to the various groups will be key to building lasting relationships and maintaining customer business because it will be unique and different. The majority of banks will still be lumping all customers into one age category.

The mature market customer base is very diverse. Understanding and marketing to the various sub-groups could spell the difference between success and failure in building unique retail strategies that differentiate one group from another.

The mature market should be divided into two major segments—pre-retirees and retirees. Within each of those two major segments are important sub-groups, as shown below:

A. Pre-retirees—age 50-64
   1. Affluent pre-retirees
B. Retirees— age 65 and over
   1. Affluent retired
   2. 75-plus households

A third, overlapping segment that should not be ignored is mature women.

Pre-Retiree Segment

Generally speaking, individuals in the 50-64 age group have a 10 percent higher income than the national average. Most of the earnings are not from wages; 66 percent earn from self-employment and over 125 percent more from estates, trusts, dividends and real estate rentals. According to the September, 1987 *American Demographics* article entitled "How Older Americans Spend Their Money": "This group pays 14 percent more taxes than the average household and nets 11 percent more after-tax income. Households headed by 55-64 year olds spend 3 percent more than the average on entertainment. This group of active Americans is now focusing their time on experiences like dining, travel, and art. They are now hiring people to take care of mundane household work like care and maintenance of the lawn and home, rather than doing it themselves."

This segment is very involved with the community, their family and their friends. They read more newspapers and magazines than any other group. They like television documentaries, PBS and "60 Minutes," "Bill Cosby," "Murder, She Wrote," and TV game shows. They tend to remain in the same geographic area and do not expect to be transferred by their employers. Should their company relocate, they will not move, but will find other employment.

Financially, their assets are highly liquid, except for their primary residence. They are at an age where accumulating assets for retirement is a priority. They are rate sensitive and risk averse. This group is ideologically traditional and fiscally and politically conservative.

When shopping they tend to favor products with guarantees and will often decide in favor of one over another based on their perception of the guarantee.

Because they are nearing retirement, they have an overwhelming concern over the safety of their savings and investment accounts and the soundness of their financial service providers. They prefer insured financial accounts. They are well-read about the financial service industry's problems. The situation with savings and loans has them very concerned and they are beginning to take their money out of these accounts to find a more secure alternative. This market segment is the "empty-nesters." The children's education is paid for or soon will be, and they are now concentrating on themselves for the first time in a long time. One of their biggest fears is that they will outlive their financial nest egg. They are also beginning to be very concerned about their own continued good health.

This segment may not be ready to take full advantage of the "club" atmosphere offered with a membership program at the bank. They would, however, be extremely receptive to participating in programs that would help them become better prepared to face a time when they are not going to be working. They want to know what options are available to them at this time in their life: everything from a new career, to educational opportunities, to planning their investment strategies more carefully.

Many investment firms, insurance companies and corporations are providing this segment with retirement seminars. It would be prudent for the bank to provide customers with retirement-related information in a subtle form. This could be done with a personal letter from the bank president letting the customer know about the new investment opportunities the bank can provide. A newsletter designed specifically for this segment would be well received. Seminars in pre-retirement related topics would be an excellent service to this segment. The topics should not only deal with the financial needs, but address housing, transitions, work alternatives, and education opportunities they might want to explore.

John Hancock Financial Services' "Real Life, Real Answers" campaign does an excellent job with 30-second television commercials showing different individuals seeking retirement advice. One particular message shows a 37-year old professional football player wondering what his retirement options would be at this stage in his life. It is not always necessary to show older people facing this transition.

This group is also referred to as the "sandwich generation"; that is, they are often taking care of aging parents and still have dependent children at home. According to AARP, over 92 percent of the women in this age category have become caregivers, looking after someone who is older. It could be as simple as taking Mom to the doctor for regular check-ups, or as complex as dealing with a parent who has moved into the household and requires constant care.

Members of this segment do not want to be reminded that they are getting older, because they simply do not feel older. They have arrived at a point in their life where they like being catered to. This group would respond to champagne breakfasts featuring highly regarded investment authorities, providing tips, hints and recommendations for wise investing.

They would be inclined to hear a noted economist discuss what is predicted for interest rates and the state of the worldwide economy.

This group is well-read and avid viewers of such popular PBS shows as the MacNeil-Lehrer Report, Louis Rukeyser's "Wall Street Week in Review" and Adam Smith's "Money World." A bank could gain great favor with this group if it sponsored a series of celebrity luncheons to hear well-known authors or popular PBS personalities.

SRI International's Values and Lifestyle Program developed a comparison of pre-retirees and the retired market published as "New Values and Lifestyles: Implications for J.C. Penney." According to the study, pre-retirees have the following financial tasks:

- Consolidating financial assets
- Providing for additional future security
- Reevaluating methods of intended property transfer
- Investigating part-time income or volunteer work for retirement
- Meeting responsibilities for aging partners and other dependents

Pre-retirees' common financial errors include:

- Lack of supplemental retirement funds
- Inadequate pensions and Social Security income
- Failure to adjust insurance coverage
- No will or out-of-date will
- Lack of knowledge about or use of community resources
- Failure to explore alternatives and options in advance of retirement

The desired retirement outcome for pre-retirees includes:

- Realistic understanding of retirement situation (economic and social)
- Knowledge of retirement income at different age levels
- Alternative sources of retirement income arranged
- Savings, protection and investment programs updated
- Revised estate plan and wills

Affluent Pre-Retirees

The affluent pre-retired sub-group only makes up 5 ½ percent of the adult population, but has extraordinary buying power. They have three times as many second homes as the general populace. More than 57 percent own American cars made in the past year, compared to 37 percent of the general population. They are active users of the preferred major credit cards; in fact, 71 percent use them compared to 46 percent for the general population.

This sub-group loves to travel. For domestic travel, 36 percent have used commercial airlines in the past year, compared to 21 percent of the general population. They are becoming investors. They lead in stock market trades 11 percent to 3 percent; bonds, 8 percent to 2 percent; mutual funds, 7 percent to 2 percent; CDs, 10 percent to 4 percent; and IRA/Keogh accounts, 53 percent to 25 percent.

That means that the 5 ½ percent that makes up this market sub-group buys 25 percent or more of all financial services.

These households are particularly concerned about protecting the real value of their savings, and they indicate a high interest in savings products that tie the interest rate to money market rates.

According to SRI, the asset protection needs of pre-retired affluent households shift as these households age, but they remain strong. The need for life insurance decreases as the children of these households leave home. Although the incidence of both group and individual life insurance remains high, it has been a median of 14 years since the most recent purchase. The incidence of property/casualty insurance, health insurance, disability insurance and professional liability insurance in this segment are higher than average. Protection of assets and the household's income is important to these households, largely because of their financial status as they approach retirement.

Households in this sub-group are generally satisfied with their financial position. They are characterized by their stability. Only five percent of them moved in the past year, and they are less likely than the average household to have had their incomes rise or fall substantially.

Individuals in this category feel that they have experience and wisdom, and they desire to share their knowledge with others. They feel society has been good to them and they want to give back to society. They will participate in focus groups or in panel discussions, sharing their experiences and life's good fortune with others.

Caution should be exercised as more and more bank marketers target the highly-sought-after affluent pre-retirees. As Leonard L. Berry, professor of Marketing at Texas A & M University, states in the 1987 *American Banker* Consumer Survey, "Chasing the affluent is an unwise policy for most retail banks. Everyone else is doing it, which makes for a hell of a lot of competition. The affluent are a difficult market to capture because they are more inclined to haggle over rates."

Retired Segment

Overall, the retired 65-74 segment consists of over 17 million consumers. By the year 2015 this age segment will expand by 45 percent.

This segment is now free to pursue things in life that they had to postpone while raising families and managing careers. Many in this segment are anxious to return to college to pursue a degree in a field that has been of lifelong interest. They want to learn and be retrained. Members of this segment are willing to actively participate in the bank's special membership programs and activities.

The average income of this segment is only two-thirds of the national average. Wages and salaries for this group are less than one-fourth of the national average. The major source of income for this group is Social Security and other retirement benefits. This group spends less in restaurants, and some of their leisure time is spent looking for discounts and sales.

This group is mixed—some that looked forward to retirement are now finding themselves unfulfilled by the retired lifestyle; they may miss the hustle and bustle of the workday world. They may end up going back to work because it offers a new and more challenging opportunity. For some this is an unsettling time. Many are becoming entrepreneurs. Nine percent of businesses in the United States are founded by people who say they are retired. Retirees are the number one group for participation in volunteer activities.

Health and well-being continue to play a major role for this segment. They are in the active stage of their retirement years and they look for ways to remain active.

Once they have settled into and adjusted to retirement, they view this phase of life as good. In fact, most are busier and more involved now than before they retired. They have more leisure time for travel. They are not as concerned about money as they were during their pre-retired stage in life.

They have a great deal of compassion for others and concern for world conditions. And they are the most active in politics and understanding political issues.

SRI International's "New Values and Lifestyles: Implications for J.C. Penney" summarizes their financial situation as follows:

Retirees' financial tasks:

- Reevaluating and adjusting living conditions and spending as they relate to health and income
- Evaluating and adjusting programs for increasing risks
- Securing reliable assistance in managing personal and economic affairs
- Finalizing plan for sharing estate
- Finalizing letter of last instruction

Retirees' common financial errors:

- Failure to consider lifestyle alternatives
- Failure to maximize group power in the marketplace
- Failure to identify and use community resources
- Failure to adjust spending to true economic situation
- Failure to develop and implement a plan for sharing the estate
- Failure to recognize and accept the interdependency of self and others and to seek help as needed
- Failure to write letter of last instructions
- Failure to finance leisure activities

Retirees' desired retirement outcome:

- Satisfactory adjustment to change in retirement income
- Use of consumer knowledge and skills and community resources maximized
- An orderly plan for transfer of property provided
- Appropriate health care, liability coverage, and supplemental income provisions made

Affluent Retired

The affluent retired aged 65-74 are considered to be movers, doers and participators. They are very secure with their financial situation. Consequently, they travel more often. They look for socially rewarding outside activities. This group provides the largest number of volunteers to the many civic, arts, health and educational agencies.

They constantly want to sharpen their minds and can be found taking courses at universities and continuing education programs, or even getting new degrees in fields they have always had an interest in.

This sub-group continues to stay very involved with and interested in making their savings and investments grow. They are interested in providing for family members and ensuring that the grandchildren will never have to worry about a college education.

They are out of the house and into the gardens, at the malls, at the ball parks or traveling to faraway lands. They hold a common view of the essential elements for maintaining quality of life and the preservation of their independence and self-reliance: connectedness, being active and feeling productive.

75-Plus Households

Americans aged 75 and over are the smallest but most rapidly growing segment of the mature market, according to the *American Demographics,* September, 1987 article "How Americans Spend Their Money." Households headed by people 75 and older have only half the income of the average households. Wages and salaries are only 6 percent of the average. They pay one-third of the taxes of the average household. This segment is more likely to begin to experience deteriorating health. In fact, *American Demographics* reports that their health care expenditures average $1,487 a year, which is 65 percent greater than those of the average household, and amounts to fully 13 percent of the total expenditures for households in this category.

They may begin to look for alternative housing that includes continuing care facilities. Those financial institutions looking to provide new services would do well to position the reverse mortgage program to this market segment, since many are house rich and cash poor.

People aged 75-plus are inclined to give more money to charities, foundations, and causes than the average household: $878 a year compared with $740 for the average household.

This segment is still very interested in maintaining a keen mind— they are avid readers and depending on their health are more likely to travel to places rich in history.

Adults in the 75-plus segment rely on advice and guidance from their personal banker. Their families are also more often involved in major financial decisions. These older adults expect their bank to possess confidence and exude security when managing savings programs.

Banks interested in developing new products should explore the benefits of developing financial products that would enable the 75-plus customer to help adult children or grandchildren fulfill family responsibilities. College funds, down payments for the purchase of a home, and expanded trust fund programs for family members would appeal to this segment.

The Mature Woman

As the number of mature market consumers increases, the women's market is growing almost as fast. This includes women with different marital statuses—the empty nest wife, women who never married, and those who are separated, divorced or widowed.

The November, 1987 "AARP News Bulletin" reported, "In 1979, American women had extended their advantage to 7.8 years with a life expectancy of nearly 78 to a man's 70." It goes on to report the gap is narrowing to 7.1 years. Women will outnumber men 2 to 1 after age 85, so they are more likely than elderly men to be widowed. Table 1 summarizes these statistics.

Table 1—Marital Status of Older Men and Women

	Age 55-64		Age 65-74		Age 75+	
	Men	Women	Men	Women	Men	Women
Percent in Category:						
Single	5	4	5	5	4	6
Married, spouse present	83	66	80	49	67	3
Married, spouse absent	2	2	2	2	2	1
Widowed	4	17	9	39	24	67
Divorced	6	9	4	5	2	3

Source: U.S. Bureau of the Census, Current Population Survey, March 1984.

In 1987, women made up 60 percent of the 65-plus population. By the year 2000, more than 19 million women will make up a large majority of our older population, and by 2020, almost 40 million women will be 65 or older. Women have received little attention from banks to help them plan for the transition to retirement, which has been perceived as a male province in which women play only a supportive and secondary role.

According to an article written by Christopher L. Hayes, Ph.D., in the March 1989 *Profit Sharing* magazine, entitled "Pre-retirement Planning Not for Husbands Only," women's retirement needs differ from those of men because the sexes age differently in our society. Women live longer, are poorer and are more likely to be widowed and living alone. When women outlive their spouses, they must stretch smaller incomes over longer lifetimes—every penny of retirement income becomes critically important. Hayes says, "Work experiences are different. Women enter the labor force later than men, have shorter work histories because of family responsibilities, have less education and job training, and often receive little or no pension coverage—in 1987, only 20 percent of women older than 65 received income from pensions."

In 1985, an AARP-commissioned Gallup survey revealed that women are more inclined to remain in the work force, delaying retirement. This in many instances is a result of the empty nest, women returning to work after the family has grown and finding great satisfaction with employment. In addition, many women age 65-plus simply must continue working because they need to support themselves.

Bank marketers would be wise to provide financial planning advice geared to women in the different 50-plus age groups. They have a tremendous need for financial information that is quite different from the needs of men. Properly done, information on how to take control of their lives and how to be better prepared to deal with the death of a spouse is one of the most invaluable services a bank could provide.

Banks should help this group better understand such financial basics as determining their net worth and understanding their financial options, and provide the necessary guidelines to help them enjoy a meaningful and productive retirement.

Society still tends to view women aged 65-75 more stereotypically than other older groups. A substantial number of women aged 65-75 are more keenly aware of financial management than most marketers realize.

Women appreciate the personal touch and person-to-person service in all banking relationships. One bank found that offering a free brochure on coping with the death of a spouse raised deposits significantly. Another highly regarded service that many women will participate in is bank-organized group travel programs.

Like everyone else in the mature market they are interested in the safety and soundness of their financial institution. They, too, are growing very concerned about the safety of their savings dollars held in savings and loan accounts.

Using Mature Market Segmentation

Segmenting the 50 and over market can be a powerful tool to help the bank become more market-driven. Be sure to conduct adequate segmentation research to help shape the programs, services, communications and products for this diverse market group.

As you enhance or build your bank marketing program targeted to people over 50, first learn all that you can about the statistics in your market. Find out what percentage of the customer base is 50-64, 65-74, women over 50 and 75-plus.

Many banks are targeting only the affluent pre-retired market segment. The bank marketer must ask if it is a sound marketing objective to direct all emphasis to the affluent older customer at the cost of omitting the secure middle income retired customer.

Senior retail management understanding and commitment to the various segments within the mature market is definitely a must. The senior program will require additional resources as well as changes in management philosophies and employee attitudes, but will provide increased deposits and stimulate the use of bank services.

An article appearing in a recent issue of the *Journal of Retail Banking,* entitled "An Appraisal of the Senior Citizen Market Segment," by John J. Burnett and Robert E. Wilkes, provides the following conclusions:

> Few profitable market segments have been built around a single variable. Although age may be a valid starting point, other related characteristics should be identified as well, such as other demographics, income, attitudes, lifestyles and bank-related factors. The latter example is particularly important since the value of a market segment is proportionate to its applicability to the business in question. It is important to determine how people in various age groups use bank products and services, how often and under what conditions.

Second, consider how this information matches the bank's current and potential product mix, pricing strategy, promotions strategy, and means of distribution. Do the affluent elderly really need reverse mortgages? Do the active elderly appreciate innovative attempts at making the products and services more convenient, or do they enjoy the social experience of visiting their local bank? The elderly may neither need nor want the discounts offered on certain bank products. Some older people may actually be embarrassed by the various benefits offered this age group. Few groups like to be highlighted in such a manner. Should advertising emphasize this age distinction or attempt a more subtle approach? These are just a few of the questions to be answered.

Third, this assessment should be considered in light of the overall bank objectives. Considering the traumatic changes taking place in the banking industry, retaining a variety of specialty programs may not be profitable. Can the modern bank still be all things to all people?

Finally, it is clear that the elderly of today may be quite different from those a decade ago, not to mention those a decade from now. Continuous monitoring and reassessment is necessary.

Our Recommendations

- ☐ Recognize that the mature market is not homogeneous. Their values and needs are not the same across all age groups or from one generation of older people to the next.

- ☐ The bank marketer should consider the values of a particular age cohort as they relate to bank products and services.

- ☐ Look to expand bank services and products to the various mature market segments beyond the club membership programs—be innovative and creative. Look to upscale promotions.

- ☐ Be sure advertising and promotional messages are also targeted to mature market segments, e.g. a special newsletter to pre-retirees on saving and investment information.

- ☐ Develop and reposition bank products to meet the various needs of the segments, e.g. grandparent's funds or loans to help other family members, college funds and down payments for homes.

- ☐ Constantly monitor the changing demographics of the mature market. Stay current with the the bank's statistics on customer habits and behavior.

- ☐ Realize that the mature market continues to change. Conduct regular customer research to make sure the program is on target with needs.

3 Researching the Market

Common Mistakes

1 Bypassing the research step and going right to program development.

2 Not placing enough value on the mature customer base to appropriate the necessary funds to conduct any qualitative or quantitative research.

3 Conducting inadequate focus group research with an unskilled moderator.

4 Cutting corners by doing a limited amount of research or only subscribing to a research service that does not identify mature market trends in the bank's trading area.

5 Failing to provide for ongoing market research after the program is launched to determine degree of satisfaction or dissatisfaction with the mature market program.

Research is a natural first step that should be taken before beginning or redesigning a marketing program targeted to the bank's mature customer base. Of course a program can be put into place without research and it can be successful. However, what we find is that bank marketing programs are improved through the judicious use of research. A great deal is learned from the data about the subtleties and nuances of the market, which ultimately helps guide the program.

In fact, gathering data is key to designing the packages and services that will attract older customers to the bank and meet the profitability goals of the bank.

Banks with successful mature customer programs will want to regularly conduct research to monitor the performance of the program. This includes conducting ongoing market research studies and obtaining monthly tracking information that provides accurate readings of the overall performance.

Our telephone interviews with banks that have already implemented programs targeted to mature customers revealed that research provided the necessary information to support the budget to establish a club or membership program. For example, Premier Bank in Baton Rouge, Louisiana, conducted focus group research to get feedback from older customers on their feelings about banking relationships, which helped Premier Bank create the Premier Partners program.

As expected, the quality of the research conducted prior to launching a program was varied. The majority of the banks interviewed said they did conduct qualitative research, such as focus groups, but less than one percent indicated that they did any quantitative research.

29

Several banks in our survey indicated that they subscribed to and purchased a number of packaged research studies that provide information on the older market segment. These reports include studies from SRI, Simmons Market Research Bureau, the Daniel Yankelovich Group, and the Council on Financial Competition.

In addition, several of the larger banks went further—commissioning outside research studies or having their advertising agencies conduct focus group sessions and other qualitative studies.

An Opportunity to Understand Behavior

The focus group provides an environment that allows for in-depth discussion of participants' reactions to financial services, memberships, and attitudes toward the bank.

Before any bank marketer launches a senior program, he or she should conduct focus groups to better understand the differences and the reasons for these differences between the various segments within the mature market customer base. For example, the marketer may feel that an 800 telephone number for discounted travel would be a needed program ingredient. Research on this issue may show that it is not critical to the bank's program—that individuals want a "human touch" by visiting a travel agent in person.

According to Gerald Sword, senior vice president and partner in Reichman/Karten/Sword, a New York City based research firm, "Focus groups used in conjunction with a survey can be an optimum method to provide banks with the information they need. However, rather than using focus groups at the beginning of a project, as is commonly done, I advise using them following a quantitative survey to 'flesh out' the statistical data. In this manner, data projectable to an entire population provides the definition and scope of a target audience, while focus groups provide the opportunity to explore in detail the reasons for identified customer attitudes."

How to Find and Develop a Focus Group

Older bank customers can usually be found in the bank's records. If invited they are often happy to participate in a focus group to tell you what they like about the bank and its services and what they do not like.

Be sure to offer an incentive for their participation. This can include a special lunch or it can include cash, usually $15 to $25 per person.

It is also important that the bank obtain information from non-customers. Church groups are great sources for people who can provide non-customer interviews. Depending on the bank's market share, it is likely that several church representatives will be bank customers as well.

Local service clubs, like Rotary, Kiwanis, etc. may provide a group that is interested in participating and choose to donate the money to a favorite charity. It is also possible to find interviewees at seniors organizations, such as R.S.V.P., the Older Women's League, and senior centers.

Most large cities, and some smaller ones, have marketing research firms which will have trained moderators on their staffs. Many of these can also recruit groups of individuals for the bank to contact. Check with others in the banking industry to find a good market research firm in your area. Also check with BMA and ABA for information they may have about reliable market research firms.

What Information Do You Seek?

When conducting focus group interviews it is important to ask the right questions to get open and honest answers to help guide the marketing strategy. Here is a list of questions bank marketers may wish to ask:

To understand the feelings of growing older:

How do you feel about getting older?

What surprises you most about being older?

(For retirees only) How do you manage your time now that you are retired?

How have your buying habits changed?

(For retirees) Do you spend more time shopping for the best deal or best interest rate now that you are retired?

What are your primary health concerns?

(For pre-retirees) What kinds of career alternatives are you exploring as retirement approaches?

(For pre-retirees) What kind of information would be helpful to you at this time of possible career transition?

What health and fitness information would be helpful to you?

To understand the sense of belonging and connectedness:

What organizations do you belong to?

Do you belong to AARP?

What do you like best about your membership in AARP?

What AARP services do you use?

What credit unions do you belong to?

What do you like best about your credit union membership?

What bank membership programs do you belong to?

What do you like best about your bank membership program?

If XYZ Bank were to offer you a membership package, what services would you like to see included in the package?

To understand how older customers perceive their banking relationships:

Describe how effective you think your primary bank (define primary bank) is at communicating with you.

What kinds of communications would you like to receive from your bank?

Based on where you are at this stage of your life, what kind of financial information would be most helpful to you?

How do you feel about the services and benefits you receive from your bank?

What advice would you give to the bank to improve that service?

To find out what services would have the greatest appeal:

Would you take advantage of premiums or special promotions offered by a bank to customers depositing $5,000 or more?

What kinds of premiums or packages are most appealing to you?

What would motivate you to change your banking relationship?

If the bank were to organize a series of trips for members of XYZ bank, what group tours would be most appealing to you?

What kind of retirement related information would be most helpful to you at this time?

What seminar topics would you find helpful to you as you approach retirement?

If XYZ Bank were to provide a special newsletter to you on a monthly basis, what kind of information would you like to see included in the articles?

To receive special membership privileges and benefits, what would be an acceptable entry level requirement? ($5,000, $10,000, or $20,000 deposit)

If the bank provided a membership services package to you with the following features (describe features) would you fulfill the necessary requirements to belong to the program, and take advantage of the membership benefits?

What would motivate you to move money from a savings account to a bank-sponsored membership program?

At this point in your life, what do you look for in the way of services from your bank?

One Bank's Focus Group Summaries

Wendy Huck, vice president of market research and management at Valley National Bank, Phoenix, who also served on the BMA Research and Planning Council, has conducted a number of focus group sessions for Valley National with seniors. Valley National discovered four attributes that were consistent from group to group—irrespective of age, income or geographic area:

- Seniors expect stellar quality service. This includes personal, courteous, and prompt service; knowledgeable, professional employees; and even personal introductions to new employees

- Seniors like "freebies." "Like" is not quite strong enough— "expect" or even "demand" is more appropriate. Seniors are very savvy. They know the bank is using their money to make money, and they expect the bank to show its appreciation by providing "things."

- Safety and security are vital to seniors. They know what FDIC insurance is. They also know what is happening to S&Ls. And, although as a group they are rate sensitive, they'd just as soon get a little less return on their investment and know their money is safe.

- Seniors like banks. They think selecting a bank is one of the most important decisions a person ever makes. Furthermore, they consider bank employees to be good sources of financial advice and truly value the working relationship they've established with their bank. Seniors prefer doing business with the well-established "local" bank, not the new bank in town.

Other research findings from the Valley National focus groups include the following general observations:

- Seniors don't think it's wise to buy on credit, but will (and do) use credit cards as a convenience.

- The appeal of personal contact increases with age.

- The importance of ATMs decreases with age.

- Seniors are more likely to read statement stuffers.

- The likelihood of reading ads increases with age.

- Seniors are much more likely to respond to surveys, fortunately for those in research.

Quantitative Research

Remember, focus group information cannot be used to make projections. Focus groups provide information on how people really feel and interact with one another in the group.

To be able to make projections and inferences about the spending habits of all people aged 50-64 requires that quantifiable data be obtained.

Quantitative research methods can be accomplished in one of three ways: questionnaires which are mailed to a selected group of individuals to be sampled; telephone interviews that also represent selective sampling; and face-to-face interviews.

David Reichman, president of Reichman, Karten and Sword, the New York City based market research firm, has conducted a number of studies on the mature market segment for the International Association of Financial Planners, in addition to conducting a number of the *American Banker* consumer studies.

Reichman prefers to use telephone interviews when obtaining quantitative data from the mature market consumer. He advises those considering telephone surveys to take into consideration the diversity of the market segment. People 50 and over represent both workers and non-workers. Therefore, it is important to obtain a good representative sample in order for the data to be meaningful.

Reichman said, "If you make your calls during the day, your sampling will consist of retired people and shift people who are at home. The retired people are very willing to participate in telephone surveys provided that they know the survey is legitimate. They are very security oriented and do not want to think the survey is a setup to determine if they are home. They have great fears of being robbed. It is important to set up the survey in a professional manner, by letting them know in advance that they will be receiving a call. This can be done with a post card informing them about the project and alerting them to expect a call. When calling individuals that work it is best to do so after work hours. Again it is important to let the individual know in advance that a survey call will be coming. Generally working people have less time to spend answering questionnaires," said Reichman. "It is important to ask the same questions, but do so with a little faster pace, so as not to take too much of their time," Reichman added.

Mail surveys are also excellent ways to obtain quantitative data. Caution should be taken when selecting the survey sample to ensure all segments of the mature market are covered to enable inferences to be made.

Sample Quantitative Questionnaire

XYZ Bank is interested in improving its services to customers. In order to make changes and improvements we need your help and input. Please take a few minutes to fill out the questionnaire and return it in the enclosed envelope.

1. How would you rate the overall service you are currently receiving from your primary bank? (Primary bank is defined as the place where you have your checking account.)

_____ Excellent
_____ Very good
_____ Good
_____ Fair
_____ Poor

2. Do you currently have savings accounts, IRAs or any other investments at other financial institutions other than your primary bank?
_____ Yes
_____ No

2a. If you answered yes to 2, are these savings or investment accounts with:
_____ Savings bank
_____ Commercial bank
_____ Credit union
_____ AARP
_____ Investment firm

2b. What is your reason for having savings accounts at institutions other than your primary bank?
_____ Better rate
_____ Better service
_____ Packaged with other benefits
_____ More convenient
_____ Investment firm

3. Do you belong to AARP?
_____ Yes
_____ No

3a. If you answered yes to question 3, please rank the following services and benefits provided by AARP with number 1 being the one you like best, 2 second, etc.
_____ Modern Maturity Magazine
_____ Legislative clout
_____ Travel discounts and trips
_____ Discount pharmacy services
_____ Entitles me to other discounts
_____ Financial and insurance service packages

4. If your primary bank were to provide you with a special membership program, which services would be most important to you? Please rank the following with number 1 being most important, 2 second, etc.
_____ Seminars on retirement related topics
_____ Group travel
_____ Discount pharmacy services
_____ Special newsletter or magazine
_____ Free checking, free travelers checks and free safe deposit box
_____ An opportunity to earn more interest on savings instruments
_____ Discounts with local merchants
_____ Health insurance

5. Thinking about the last five times you conducted a bank transaction, how many were made by each of the following methods:
_____ Mail
_____ Drive-up window
_____ Going into the bank
_____ Direct deposit
_____ ATM

6. Do you find the service you are currently provided by the customer service representatives (tellers) at your primary bank to be:
_____ Friendly, personal, and professional
_____ Unfriendly, impersonal and unprofessional

7. When you go into the bank to conduct a transaction, do you generally find the following:
_____ Fast and immediate service
_____ Convenient hours and convenient location
_____ Immediate access to tellers
_____ Personal service to meet your every financial need

8. Would the following information be helpful to you at this time? Rank in order of importance with number 1 being most important, 2 second, etc.
_____ How to maintain today's financial lifestyle into retirement
_____ Savings and investment instruments that yield safety and high interest
_____ Housing options and choices in retirement
_____ Health, fitness and nutrition advice
_____ Career and educational opportunities in retirement

9. At this point in your life, would you like to know your:
_____ Net worth
_____ Investment risk tolerance
_____ Anticipated health insurance costs
_____ Financial plan for retirement

10. Would you like your primary bank to provide the following? Please rate with number 1 being most desirable, number 2 second, etc.
_____ A personal banker
_____ Personal banking at home
_____ Senior coordinator to answer retirement related questions

Thank you for taking the time to answer these questions. We appreciate your input.

Other Sources of Information

Other sources of information can be used to get a seniors program underway. Every state receives funds from the federal government's Administration on Aging to carry out programs and services to meet the needs of residents 60 and over. In turn, each state agency allocates funds to local entities called Area Agencies on Aging. Each agency is required to maintain data on the number, location and needs of older adults in a particular area. Your state and Area Agencies on Aging can provide valuable information. (See the Appendix for listings.)

Post-Market Research

If a bank is going to look at the mature customer's value to the bank by conducting qualitative and quantitative research prior to launching a program, it should make a similar commitment to post-market research as well.

As the marketplace becomes more competitive for deposit dollars, the astute marketer will want to conduct regular follow-up research to ensure that the customer is taking advantage of the programs offered and to make any modifications for improvement.

Our Recommendations

☐ Before designing the program, find out what mature customers want and need from their financial institution by doing market research.

☐ Use the data to plan, design and launch the program based on what the facts reveal.

☐ Pre-test advertisements before saturating the mature customer with program sign-up offers.

☐ Use both qualitative and quantitative research to get both feelings and facts.

☐ Prepare an executive summary of the survey findings for top management's review.

☐ Conduct follow-up research to ensure that the strategies are on target and to make modifications and improvements.

4 Developing the Package

Common Mistakes

1 Failure to develop and execute a strategy of capturing high-balance seniors savings and investment accounts or defending these accounts against competitive offerings.

2 Lack of understanding that the essence of the program is in the total seniors banking relationship in related savings and investment accounts.

3 Failure to understand that the offer of free checking with no monthly account charge is a necessary element in the seniors program.

4 Lack of understanding of the necessity to cross-sell accounts constantly in order to maximize the rapport established through the seniors club and take advantage of the constant growth of account balances.

5 Failure to gain the continued approval of management and the commitment to adequate research and promotional budget, designated staff, bank-wide training and sales tracking.

6 Setting levels for minimum seniors account balances that have no relationship to the competitive situation, the proportion of mature customers in the market or corporate or marketing strategies.

7 Underestimating the potential for account growth and average balances in start-up situations.

8 Choosing seniors account or package enhancements by following the market leader or using intuitive judgment not supported by research.

Banks that have targeted the mature market and established banking services for seniors through accounts or clubs are finding an unusual level of success, whether they measure their efforts in number of accounts, average balances, total balances or new money deposited with the bank. In fact, for a large number of banks it borders on the amazing.

We know of banks whose average balance per seniors account is 15 to 20 times the minimum balance. And, while average checking account balances are in the $3,000 range, the savings and investment accounts held by seniors as part of the program are likely to be in the $20,000 to $30,000 range. We know of banks that have far exceeded these numbers.

38

The Formula

What is the formula for reaching the mature market customer segment successfully? It is providing the best personal service, helping older customers prepare to make a smooth transition from the pre-retirement to the retirement stage and creating a special sense of belonging with membership packages or programs.

Why does the concept of packaged accounts appeal to the older customer? According to SRI, more than half of those in the 50-plus group are "belongers." They have a strong need at this stage of their lives to feel connected to people their own age who share similar life experiences. Bank packages, especially those with social elements, provide this sense of connection.

If there is a model in the financial services industry that comes close to creating this type of feeling, it is the credit union. The 1987 *American Banker's* annual consumer opinion survey showed that credit union members were the most satisfied consumers of financial services. One of the executive tips from the survey's section, "How To Keep Consumers Happy," revealed, "Consumers love the service, interest rates and feel of credit unions; so act more like a credit union; think family, not customer. Appeal to group loyalties with affinity programs aimed at specific ethnic groups, occupations and hobbies." Marketers in banking can create this family-like feeling by developing membership programs for customers age 50 and over. They are finding it an effective way to reach and penetrate the seniors market. The best way is not through a mass marketing approach but through a package of financial and other social services, usually marketed under the umbrella of a club.

The Packaged Account: A Short History

The concept of tailoring packages to bank customers is a marketing concept that many banks use successfully. The best known and most successful of all the packaged accounts was the Wells Fargo Gold Account introduced in the late 1970s. The account satisfied the need of bank customers for consolidation of a number of customer savings, checking and credit card accounts into a single account with a monthly fee of $2 to $3.

The concept of the Gold Account, introduced by former BMA president Richard M. Rosenberg, then marketing director for Wells Fargo and today vice chairman of Bank of America, San Francisco, swept across the country as banks elsewhere found the concept equally well received in their marketplaces.

Now, in much the same way, many banks are creating seniors banking accounts or clubs to attract those customers and prospective customers within a predetermined age group. Some have gone so far as to extend their segmentation strategy across an adult lifetime. St. Paul Federal Bank for Savings, in Chicago, has introduced its "Lifetimes" financial services package.

The program is composed of six different plans allowing customers to set financial goals as their income levels and responsibilities change. Focus group research showed that the average customer had relatively simple financial objectives, and was generally intimidated when confronted with the range of banking products.

The six plans are structured around recent college graduates or young adults in their first jobs; first-time home buyers; home owners interested in home improvements; young families with children beginning to save for college; asset-accumulating customers building toward retirement, and the near-retired and retired planning to enjoy retirement.[1]

Determining Mature Market Program Needs

Before deciding to offer a club or membership program to customers aged 50 and older, careful research should be conducted. It is important to look at the bank's existing customer base and determine the average and total balances maintained in checking accounts, savings accounts and investment products by those over 50. Since most bank customers have savings accounts at other financial institutions, it is important to monitor CD accounts that mature in 60 or 90 days.

After evaluating activity with customers over 50, the marketer needs to look to the statewide or trading area statistics of those nearing 50 or over this age level. An analysis of this nature will point out that some regions of the state have a greater concentration of older residents—important information for the bank's branch location and operation.

The next step is to look at what the competition is offering to mature customers. Competition includes banks, savings banks, savings and loan associations, credit unions, consumer credit companies and all other financial intermediaries. Do they have named clubs? Are they advertising to the market? What are the features of their clubs, both banking and other? What are the costs of the club? What is the size of their membership?

This is a critical issue in the development of strategy. The first bank or savings and loan that enters the market usually has the edge on others for some time, if they have the promotional budget to create awareness of their position. Among the banks that have been in this position are Bank of Boston, Valley National Bank in Phoenix and FirsTier Bank in Omaha. A strategy that creates a truly differentiating advantage is required by those who come into the market later.

Next, it is important to establish objectives for the program. Here are examples:

■ To establish an identity in the marketplace by which we are widely known as the predominant bank offering services to the mature market.

40

- To develop an in-bank environment for serving the seniors customer that will build strong loyalties through relationships and will minimize customer erosion to competing financial institutions.

- To increase the average bank-wide cross-sell ratio of bank products and services to two to three times its current level.

- To develop levels of profitability in serving the older customer that ensure that the bank's overall deposit, investment, trust and credit goals are achieved.

- To increase the amount of new money in savings and investment accounts by older customers.

Once the objectives have been established, it is necessary to get the approval and commitment of top management. We find that any mature market program is dependent—almost critically—on top management's continued recognition that the mature market is one of the top priorities in the retail bank. Keeping management involved in some way, e.g., recognition programs, awards, participation on trips or tours, helps maintain their enthusiasm.

Making sure that the program is positioned as part of the overall corporate goals helps. Because the numbers of accounts and members will often surpass budgeted projections, the presentation of this data to the board of directors on a regular basis can help the program carry a high profile.

An important and necessary element of the mature program is the expectation that older customers have of receiving discounts and other price breaks as part of the program. The reason for that is they receive many discounts from other businesses—hotels, airlines, brokerage firms, hospitals, insurance companies, pharmaceutical firms, drug stores, and even popular ice cream chains. They receive bonuses, awards and points as frequent flyers and frequent buyers. They are likely to be members of AARP and receive many discounted offers.

Strategies for Seniors Packages

There is certainly adequate research and data available that proves bank membership programs directed to the seniors market work. Chapter 5 details a number of specific mature market programs and their results.

The primary banking product used by almost all of the banks as the basis for a membership program is the checking or demand deposit account. It is then packaged with a number of appealing non-financial services, which are perceived by the customer to be of value to them.

Offering free checking with a minimum balance requirement appeals to the "value-needs" of the mature segment and results in many high balance customers moving their accounts to the seniors club or account.

Usually banks offer the package with a minimum balance, but minimum balances may vary widely—from $100 to as high as $50,000, in exceptional cases. For example, Premier Bank in Louisiana has a $2,500 minimum balance on its Premier Partners account. The Prime Advantage account at Society Bank in Cleveland requires a $10,000 minimum. The packaged program available from FISI, Nashville, Tenn., has a $100 minimum balance.

Determining the minimum balance level is an important strategic decision. Setting the amount will depend on the bank's marketing strategy, position in the market, the competitive situation and profit objectives. One approach is to go with a low minimum balance and attract a larger base of senior accounts. Adopting a low minimum balance strategy may be an opportunity to exploit the market. This works as long as the cost of servicing those accounts is compensated for by their deposit balances.

In actuality, a low balance may not be an advantage, because even low balances bring average balances 20 to 30 times larger than the minimum. Another approach is to maintain a high minimum and attract those who can afford higher balances. This is based on the belief that a higher minimum helps increase the bank's profitability in the short term.

Frequently, seniors programs result in consolidated balances as much as three times larger than other types of general programs offered to customers at large.

The Perceived Benefits of Packaging

It is easy to see why seniors banking services or seniors clubs are beneficial to many banks. But why are they perceived by customers as being so valuable? The reason is in the psychological, social and economic make-up of the older bank customer. As discussed in earlier chapters, a seniors package or club membership can meet the needs of a consumer who is in a "life-satisfying" stage.

This person is more concerned with enjoying life, providing counsel to others through his or her experiences and avoiding loneliness and other fears. And the person enjoys being given the attention, privileged status and fellowship of a club. These people want to belong and have a need to be a part of something they can relate to. Those banks operating successful, enduring programs clearly recognize this need and respond to it.

At the same time, marketers should understand that the mature market doesn't like to pay for what it doesn't use. A package of banking and non-banking services perceived to be part of the cost of belonging to a seniors club will not be well received by older customers.

"Special packages are something that banks are almost obliged to offer seniors," says Margie Kane, marketing officer of the $9 billion Philadelphia National Bank. The bank's "Seniority Account" program has 3,400 members. "Seniors make up a market that no one has paid a lot of attention to for a lot of years but now they have to and they are."[2] Echoes

42

Janet Haffner, personal banking officer at the $91 million Heritage Bank, Blue Island, Illinois,[3] "The big thing in running a club is loving your people to death. Most of these people are extremely lonely."

Heritage offers 2,500 members an array of benefits—free checking, direct deposit of Social Security checks, an ATM card, safe deposit box discounts and personal financial consultation to those maintaining $2,500 in savings or NOW accounts or a combined balance of $10,000 in any of the bank's investment accounts. Other benefits include tours, a newsletter, a membership card with a photo of the member and merchant discounts.

In an unusual twist and one that generates income, the bank accepts associate members who may not be customers but who pay $150 a year to receive many of the club's benefits such as free traveler's checks and money orders, photocopying privileges and participation in the club's social activities. Each month the bank rents a local theater and shows classic movies for just a 10-cent admission. On several occasions 1,700 people have shown up for the movie.

Bank-Centered Versus Product-Centered Seniors Marketing

"Banks can bundle and cross-sell services in countless ways, but a promotional effort aimed at the seniors market calls for a different kind of relationship banking," says Robert F. Collins, Jr., vice president-marketing, Bank Five for Savings, Burlington, Massachusetts.[4]

"Any bank planning a seniors program must break away from 'product thinking' and promote a way of bank-centered living among its mature customers. Market research and Bank Five's experience shows that free and discounted bank services are much less important to mature customers than the social opportunities offered in a program such as The Presidential Group."

As an example, in the first year of the program, targeted to those 50 and older, the bank sponsored four cocktail parties, four dinner/theater parties, an investment seminar and trips to New York City and Bermuda. Collins says the opportunities are not limited to group trips or parties but include any aspect of the program that brings people together to learn, to be entertained and to enjoy the company of others.

The point Collins makes is a valid one for others who are interested in beginning programs. The social aspects provide continuity and encourage employees to build relationships with customers, reinforcing loyalty which generally results in larger deposits and the use of other banking services.

Elements of the Seniors Account

The typical seniors account consists of any or all of the following:

- Checking Services
  - Free demand deposit accounts
  - Free negotiable orders of withdrawals (NOW accounts)
  - Free printing of checks
  - Free traveler's checks
  - Free money orders
  - Free Treasury checks

- Credit Services
  - Credit card
  - Debit card (ATM)
  - Personal lines of credit
  - Vehicle loans
  - First mortgage loans
  - Second mortgage loans
  - Mobile home loans
  - Check overdraft protection

- Savings and Investment Services
  - Passbook savings account
  - Certificates of deposit
  - Individual Retirement Accounts
  - Statement savings

- Other Banking Services
  - Trust services
  - Free safe deposit boxes
  - Direct deposit of payroll or Social Security checks
  - Discount brokerage
  - Check-cashing cards
  - Check verification cards

- Insurance Services
  - Accidental death insurance

- Educational Services
  - Pre-retirement seminars
  - Personal financial planning seminars
  - Newsletters on financial, health, lifestyle issues
  - Magazines
  - Booklets
  - Flyers

- Medical Discounts
  - Prescription pharmacy services
  - Veterinarian services

- Merchants' Discounts
  - Garden supplies
  - Horticulturists
  - Automobile repair stores
  - Restaurants
  - Theaters

- Travel-Related Services
  - Local or regional attractions
  - Day trips
  - Ocean cruises

- Memberships in Other Programs
  - Club or account membership cards
  - American Association of Retired Persons
  - State or local senior citizen programs

- Personal Services
  - Document copying services
  - Notary public services
  - Key-ring registration

Old Versus New Money

Many of the clubs and account packages do an effective job in developing awareness with current bank customers and getting them to join their club or packaged account. Upwards of 66 to 85 percent of the dollars come from accounts already with the bank. This is due in part to how a seniors program starts. It begins with the bank marketing to its own customers about the account. The result is that the dollars are moved from existing accounts to the seniors account.

Frequently, the pattern is that existing accounts grow by as much as 10 percent over the next 12 to 24 months. New money, on the other hand, usually has average balances much lower than those of existing customers.

Once it is launched and established, the seniors program must do three things:
1. Develop appropriate cross-selling tactics to expand the size of the accounts, gain new ones and attract new money from other banking relationships the mature customer has. Research shows that mature customers hold as many as three other major savings accounts.
2. Use the existing base of mature customers to provide referrals to those outside the bank. The older customer relies heavily on the opinion of those in their age group in making decisions.
3. Use the promotional budget to aggressively seek new dollars.

An example of a bank that does an exceptional job of expanding its seniors total accounts and balances is Barnett Banks in Jacksonville, Florida. By skillfully marketing its pre-eminent position, it takes advantage of its presence in a booming seniors market which averages 2,000 persons moving to Florida each day. The bank offers a combination of services that allows almost anyone to join and aggressively courts new dollars through marketing communications in those states in the Midwest and North where a high percentage of seniors relocate to Florida.

Extraordinary Cross-Sell Ratios

Depending on the package the bank chooses to offer, there is an exceptionally high cross-sell ratio with older customers who participate. While the industry ratio of accounts per household is about two accounts per household per bank, those with seniors programs that cross-sell aggressively have closer to five to six accounts per household.

Older persons tend to have more than one account relationship with a bank. If they have a number of accounts with the bank it becomes easier to cross-sell more banking services. National banking statistics show the increasing levels of loyalty to an institution with an increasing number of accounts. For example, a customer with eight to ten accounts with the bank is a customer for life unless he or she moves or a major servicing catastrophe occurs at the bank.

Unfortunately, only a limited number of banks track their mature market account or club in a meaningful way. This factor makes the measurement of the program dependent only on account balances and number of accounts participating.

An Example of a Launch

A combination of research, understanding the market and timing makes for a successful launch. Fourth Financial Corporation, Wichita, Kansas, determined through market research and studying other successful banks that a packaged product with a number of relationships would best meet its customer base from short-term, high-rate competitor promotions.[5] The bank organized three focus groups with young, middle-aged and older participants, with the subject of product packaging. Among the questions they were asked were:

- How many institutions are you banking with?
- What do you think of the packaging concept?
- If you could have a packaged account, what products and services would you most want?

After completing the session, the bank put together several approaches and went to senior customers of the bank for their input. Before taking it to market, the bank's marketing team researched the senior packages of 69 financial institutions in each of its markets. They found that most of the competitor accounts were simply enhanced checking accounts with the monthly service charge waived and several features added.

The bank then announced Status 55, which combined four key services with a number of benefits and bonuses tied into the package. The package included a savings account and certificates of deposit, both with a $1,000 minimum balance, a checking account and a credit card. Service charges are waived on the non-interest-bearing checking account, and there is no fee for the Visa or MasterCard. The bank purchased a program from a packaged supplier offering 20 percent rebates on air travel, lodging, car rentals, tours and cruises. Customers also receive a free estate planning consultation, free notary public services, group travel and seminars. Early on, the bank offered a $55 incentive to customers, which was added to their CD.

The bank used two employee incentive programs for Status 55: a sweepstakes program for customer service representatives and a referral contest for all other employees. More than 20 percent of the 4,300 accounts opened were attributable to employees. Of the 1,500 referrals made, 900 resulted in new Status 55 relationships. At the end of the campaign the bank had added $131 million with the average household balance of $30,000. Average cost per added account was $100.

Naming the Club or Account

Bankers are divided over the best approach to naming a seniors club or seniors package of accounts. Using age numbers in the name differentiates the account's or club's target audience from other age brackets. Examples are Orlando Sun Banks' "SunHorizon 55"; Bank of Boston's "Portfolio 55"; in Grand Rapids, Michigan, Old Kent Bank and Trust Company's "Advantage 50"; and in Boston Shawmut's "60 Plus Plan." However, some bank marketers believe the number in the name too narrowly defines the scope of the club. What happens if the bank shifts its target from age bracket 55 to 50, or even 45? While age 45 may seem low, one leading marketer told us his bank believes enduring relationships for the seniors market are best started at a lower age bracket. His bank's strategy is to "jump the market" by beginning at age 45.

As far as names go, others believe a better approach is a name like Phoenix's Valley National Bank and its "Value Partners"; Cleveland's Society Bank and its "Prime Advantage Account"; Barnett's "Senior Partners," and Mercantile Bancorporation and its "Merchantile Exclusive Senior Account."

A bank that recently changed the name of its package of banking services for older customers to allow more people to qualify is Central Fidelity Bank of Richmond. Its "Focus 60" program is now "Focus 55" and is open to bank customers 55 and older who have accounts with a minimum balance of $2,500. The group represents 40,000 households, roughly five percent of households in the bank's customer base, and 25 percent of total bank deposits.

It is our feeling that the bank should think about the name of the club or account with the following in mind:

- What is the bank's mature market definition? Could it change in the near term? What would the effect of the change be?

- What competitive names exist in the trading area today? Could an interstate merger bring a large bank with a similar name into the marketplace causing confusion? Are there advantages or disadvantages to taking a name that is similar to such a competitor?

- Have marketers asked senior bank customers what they want to call it?

Deciding Whether to Use a Turn-Key Program

The bank will need to weigh carefully the advantages and disadvantages of using a packaged or proprietary seniors program. The largest provider of mature market services in the country is FISI Madison Financial based in Nashville, Tennessee.

FISI provides a menu of mature market services to more than 500 banks. Its package includes:

- Accidental death insurance
- Credit card protection
- Discount eyewear
- Discount pharmacy service
- Emergency cash services
- Local and national discounts
- Discount shopping service
- Bonus travel programs
- Financial newsletter

FISI generally recommends that banks begin the program requiring customer/members to have a $100 minimum balance in a checking account or demand deposit. The program is designed to increase deposits, generating income from the spread and encouraging depositors to consolidate their relationships with one bank.

FISI projects a 10 percent increase in relationships from present customers who become members and a minimum eight percent new account acquisition rate. In addition, a residual amount of fee income can be expected from 14 percent of the accounts that fall below the minimum balance.

Another turn-key program, the Richer Life, requires that members maintain $20,000 in accounts of their choice. Non-members who do not have $20,000 in accounts but who wish to participate in the program can do so by paying $10 per month to receive the non-financial privileges.

Richer Life members receive free checking accounts, free personalized checks, $1,000 accidental death insurance, free travelers checks and an ATM card, along with a member photo identification card.

The non-banking services include a quarterly newsletter, "Richer Outlook," planned and coordinated group travel activities, financial planning seminars and free trust consultation at the bank or at home.

The Richer Life program emerged from Bank Five's "Presidential Group," developed by Bob Collins. The program was then franchised by Value Added Marketing's A.J. Biren, Southboro, Massachusetts. The age requirement is 50 or older. According to Collins, the program is personalized for each subscribing bank. It is designed to get savings deposits, not checking accounts.

Norwood ("Red") Pope, senior vice president/director of marketing at Valley National Bank, Phoenix, Arizona, does not use a turn-key provider. He maintains that the bank has the capability and the resources to develop, create, maintain and administer its own seniors membership program.

Judie MacDonald, vice president and manager, retail sales & products, Barnett Banks, Jacksonville, Florida, does not use a turn-key program because, after conducting extensive research for their bank, found that many of the services in the package did not prove to be as popular with customers as they would like.

On the other hand, 1st National Bank in Grand Forks, North Dakota, and FirsTier Bank in Omaha, Nebraska, find that a packaged program is a great benefit because they do not have the staff resources to commit to the administration and handling for all the non-financial services they provide. FISI was able to provide them with the necessary training for implementing the program, which included training of the president and all customer service representatives.

It is important to understand the pluses and minuses involved in either creating an original program in-house or contracting with a turn-key provider. Before making that decision, the bank may want to retain the services of an independent consultant with expertise at running successful senior membership programs.

Implementing a Seniors Program: The Marketing Plan

A comprehensive, formal marketing plan of action provides the means of bringing the elements of the package together. Those elements should include:

- A statement or series of statements that establish the objectives for the seniors program, including the bank's overall objectives.

- A list of financial products and services that will be part of the package.

- Descriptions of extra services that add value and benefits to the mature customer. Care should be taken to distinguish between benefits for the customer and the bank.

49

- Advertising and promotional strategies including how the bank will promote the program initially and thereafter.

- Communication plans that let the members and potential members know about the programs and its activities. This should include a newsletter or magazine.

- A budget including funds for on-going research, promotions, employee cash incentives, acquisition cost per member/customer.

- Description of orientation and training plans for customer contact personnel as well as senior management, sensitivity training, employee incentives for signing up customers.

- A program for referral bonuses or other incentives for members who refer others.

- A plan for monitoring and tracking results of the program, including membership listing, customer profile and periodic sales report.

- Allocation of staff time—professional and clerical, job descriptions, responsibilities and salaries.

- Timelines and strategies for introducing the program to branch offices on a phased or mass basis.

- Projected quarterly sales plan including membership sign-up and deposit growth.

Effectively Spending Promotional Dollars

Many programs are launched with a big advertising bang—then, for any number of reasons, the promotional budget is reduced. Reaching the mature market effectively takes sizable promotional dollars, especially if the plan is to gain many accounts before competitive reaction. The advertising should be tested before running. In many instances, the mature customer reacts differently than expected and pre-testing can make advertising more effective. For more details, see Chapter 7.

It may not be necessary to use expensive television ads; rather, rely on directed media such as direct mail. Letters from the bank CEO thanking mature customers for their years of loyalty and announcing the benefits of the seniors program will be well received.

The packaged program should be introduced to employees in a major way. There are a number of ways to do so that can create excitement over what this opportunity offers—employee meetings, dinners, advertising reviews, videotaped messages from the CEO, promotional events and the announcement of incentive programs for account opening referrals.

The packaging of services for bank employees can be a major opportunity to expand market share and build profitability. It requires expertise, organization and determination but the rewards can be great.

Our Recommendations

☐ Determine management's interest in committing to a seniors package that includes offering social, educational and other activities. If the response is positive, then proceed with the plans. If it is not positive, then do not try to develop the program. Without management's approval, it will not succeed.

☐ Analyze and decide whether the best approach is to a proprietary program or purchasing one from a vendor that offers a turn-key operation.

☐ Research the market before determining the minimum balance levels. Network with other banks or use external consultants to make this key decision.

☐ Set up a seniors advisory panel to help the bank determine the elements of the seniors package. Review carefully such items as retail discounts, pharmaceutical discounts and discounted travel plans.

☐ Involve all employees in the planning the package. Their support is crucial. Set aside dollars for awards, cash incentives and recognition programs for employees who refer others. Train the customer contact personnel in the elements of the package.

☐ Develop an advertising program that sells the benefits of the seniors package in a way that is meaningful for the mature market. Provide a portion of budget for internal marketing of the program and developing constant reminders for employees about the package.

Notes

1. Thomas J. Rinella, "Packaging Services to Create Added Value," *Bank Marketing,* November, 1988, P. 18.
2. "Financial Clout of Seniors Drawing Increased Attention," *Marketing Update,* Bank Marketing Association, September, 1987, P. 1.
3. "Financial Clout." Op. Cit. P. 1.
4. Robert F. Collins, Jr., "Senior Programs—A 'Golden' Opportunity to Provide Bank-Centered Lifestyles," *Bank Marketing,* March, 1988, P. 12.
5. Laurie Carney, "Strategic Offensive at Bank IV Wins Local Battle in 'Senior Wars,'" *Bank Marketing,* September, 1987, P. 23.

5 Examples of Programs That Work

Common Mistakes

1 Not having any programs or services targeted to the mature market customer base.

2 Establishing a mature market seniors' club program with insufficient budgetary support to maintain and build the program over a period of years.

3 Short term goals and not enough long range planning for program implementation beyond the initial start-up phase. Losing enthusiasm after the program's first year.

4 Failing to provide or designate adequate staff support to effectively manage the program within the bank and throughout the branch system.

5 Failing to incorporate the objectives of the program into the bank's overall corporate goals.

6 Not obtaining a commitment of support from top management for the program's ongoing support.

7 Providing a program that is personality driven and not built into the bank's corporate objectives to ensure continuity.

8 Jumping into a program without conducting adequate market research.

9 Providing poor or inadequate tracking reports to monitor the program on a regular and ongoing basis.

There are a number of pre-retirees and retirees that desire a location in a warm climate. The number one spot in the nation with the highest proportion of residents aged 65-plus is Sarasota, Florida.

According to Population Reference Bureau (PRB), a non-profit research group, 9 of the 10 metro areas with the highest senior population are in Florida. First is Bradenton with 27 percent, followed by West Palm Beach, Boca Raton, and Delray Beach with 23 percent and Fort Meyers, and Cape Coral with 22 percent.

Given these statistics, it seems only appropriate to begin with Jacksonville's Barnett Bank Senior Partners Program.

Barnett Bank, Jacksonville, Florida
Club Name: Senior Partners
Requirements: Age 55 or over, checking account plus money market account or CD
Program Launch: 1982

Services: Free checking, special checks and check book cover with program logo, cashier's checks, financial planning guide, 10 percent discount on first trade with Barnett Brokerage Service

Other Features: $100,000 common carrier accidental death insurance, free copying service, quarterly newsletter, seminars on financial planning, health and wellness

Sponsorship: Senior Olympics, golf and shuffleboard tournaments, AARP Tax Aid, the 55 Alive driving course

Barnett provides the Senior Partners program to customers and residents in the state of Florida 55 years of age and older. The program is responsible for $6.5 billion in deposits and has over 500,000 members!

The bank's promotion saturates Florida and Georgia with over 500 branches, direct mail, statement stuffers and media advertising, says Judie MacDonald, vice president of retail sales and product management.

"When we introduced Senior Partners, we made a commitment to contribute to the lifestyle needs of seniors as well as their financial needs," MacDonald says.

Senior Partners is available to those 55-plus who have a checking account and money market or certificate of deposit account at the bank.

Barnett has 33 banks and 502 branches, meaning that many of Florida's seniors have access to the programs. The branches choose which activities in the Senior Partners package to offer.

Branches sponsor local Senior Olympics, golf and shuffleboard tournaments. They provide members with seminars on topics ranging from financial planning to health and wellness, to cruises, to how to be prepared in case of hurricanes. Barnett also teams up with AARP to offer customers Tax Aid and the 55 Alive driving course.

The aggressive, informative television ad campaign features Betty White, popular star of NBC's "Golden Girls." In the 30-second TV commercial White says, "I hope Barnett's is providing the Senior Partners program years from now when I turn 55."

In addition, the bank has designated an individual to represent the needs and wants of senior citizens. The Senior Ambassador speaks to senior organizations explaining the Senior Partners range of benefits and services.

Barnett also offers the Senior Premium Account for customers with an income of $40,000 or net assets of $100,000. The customer with a Premium Account is assigned to a Personal Relationship Banker, who acts as a liaison between the customer and the various bank departments.

Valley National Bank, Phoenix, Arizona

Club Name: Value Partners, chosen to coordinate with other names Valley National Bank is using, such as Value Checking.

Program Launch: September, 1985

Requirements: Age 55 or over, demand account and time account with minimum opening balances

Services: Free checking, no-fee charge card, traveler's checks, periodic deposit premium rates

Other Features: "Experience Arizona" coupon book with a value of $3,000 for theaters, golf courses, and symphonies; quarterly newsletter

According to Red Pope, senior vice president/director of marketing at Valley National Bank, a lot of research was obtained prior to launching the Value Partners program.

Much of the data and information about the characteristics of mature banking relationships was conducted while Pope was at Sun Banks, Orlando, Florida. "We learned that the financial needs and wants of the older bank customer were not that much different from state to state," said Pope. A number of focus group interviews were conducted to get input directly from the mature customers and potential customers to find out what they wanted from the banking relationship.

The program was launched in September, 1985. To announce the program's availability and benefits, Valley National used television advertising and direct mail.

The Value Partners program is available to anyone over 55. Customers are required to have two linked accounts which include a demand account and a time account with minimum opening balances. In turn, Valley Bank provides its mature customer with free checking, no-fee charge cards, free traveler's checks, and periodic discounts and buying opportunities in the form of a coupon booklet worth $3,000 called "Experience Arizona." Senior customers can buy the book for $7.50, or it is provided to them free if they bring in a new Partner. The coupons provide discounts to golf courses, theaters, symphonies, upscale restaurants, and other attractions. According to Pope, "The booklet is very popular because it has great value to our members."

In the newsletter, two times a year, Value Partners are offered 20% discounts on anything in Goldwater's department store.

Since the program was launched, some modifications and changes were made. Pope said, "Initially we offered Value Partners a discount travel program and discounts for prescription drugs. We discontinued both services because our customers told us they would rather sit down face-to-face with their established travel agent rather than call a stranger at an 800 number."

Customers over 55 are very vocal and responsive to the program. Pope described a situation where the chairman of the board appeared on TV commercials saying that because the people at Valley National are human, there is a special customer relationship—"If we make mistakes we'll fix them." At the same time the bank was going to increase the minimum balance requirements for Value Partners to $5,000 in all linked accounts. The office was deluged with phone calls commenting on the increase; most felt it was unfair. Pope indicated that most of them already had balances over $5,000. The situation was resolved to the satisfaction of customers when the chairman of the board sent a letter to all Value Partners stating "I told you I'd fix it—I'm going to be true to my word. We should not request that of existing members. It is only for new Value Partners who sign up."

Valley Bank is the largest bank in the state, with a 34 percent share of the market. The senior program has approximately 31 percent share of the overall deposit business.

Pope said that having the first seniors program in the state helped Value Bank a great deal. "It was two years before the competition offered a like program," said Pope.

The seniors program was instituted for three reasons: 1) to attract savings; 2) the community and region attracts a lot of older residents, and 3) to retain deposit business, which according to Pope is central to the bank's success. The strategy to reach and target seniors is part of the bank's overall marketing plan.

The results have been increased deposits, greater loyalty and a more active customer membership base of more than 50,000 seniors.

Meridian Bancorp, Philadelphia, Pennsylvania

Club Name: Club 50

Program Launch: October, 1988

Requirements: Age 50 or over, $100 balance in interest paying transaction accounts

Services: Free personalized checks, discounts on safe deposit boxes, emergency cash advances

Other Features: Travel benefits, key ring registration, newsletter, free credit card protection, accidental death insurance, pharmacy discounts, travel rebates, free copying service

Meridian Bank recognized the need to start a program for customers age 50 and over after doing six months of extensive market research. The statistics revealed that Pennsylvania has the fourth largest population in the nation of residents over age 50, and data also revealed that the bank's customers had an average of $66,000 on deposit in three financial institutions other than the bank. The research also provided revealing information about customers' needs and wants. The safety of funds was found to be the primary concern for more customers age 50 and over. Customers are also vitally interested in their personal health and in travel.

In addition, Meridian was feeling competitive pressure from other banks in the state that were targeting the mature market, including Merchant's Bank in Allentown, Quakertown National Bank, First Valley in Bethlehem, Nazareth National Bank, Hazelton National Bank and United States National Bank in Johnstown.

Club 50 became the largest retail banking promotion developed by Meridian in four years. The advertising and promotion budget for the first year was $1 million, with 40 percent allocated to local television ads, 20 percent to newspapers and publications, 10 percent to radio and the remainder to cash incentives to branch personnel who open new Club 50 accounts for customers.

Club 50 has more than a dozen benefits and features, which include checking accounts that pay interest with no service fee on a minimum balance of $100, free Club 50 personalized checks, annual fee waivers on MasterCard and Visa, free credit card protection, and discounts on safe deposit boxes, travel, recreation and pharmacy service.

During the first week of kick-off, the Reading-based Meridian branch opened $28 million in new Club accounts, of which 10 percent was new money. Most of the accounts were conversions of accounts already established by Meridian customers.

Meridian has contracted with FISI Madison Financial for the non-financial services. FISI subcontracts travel services for Club 50 members to a travel agency. After a member completes an itinerary, the travel agency will reimburse a discount ranging from 3% to 10% on hotel, car rental and airline bookings made through the agency. FISI receives $1 per month per customer for the service.

The bank sees Club 50 as an opportunity to make profits by providing members with investment and trust services and by making loans.

Continental Federal Savings Bank, Fairfax, Virginia

Club Name: Senior Service Centers

Requirements: Age 55 or over, $100 minimum deposit

Services: Free checking, Senior Services Centers

Other Features: Seminars, newsletter, social outings

The Senior Service Centers established by Continental Federal Savings Bank, Fairfax, Virginia, provide seniors with their own private centers located at bank branches.

Continental Federal staffs each center with a trained counselor, a mature banking representative who provides customer service. This gives senior members someone their own age that they can identify with and relate to.

The centers are gathering places for senior members to attend weekly events that the bank sponsors. Events include seminars on topics of interest ranging from arts and crafts to bridge, to health and wellness, to wills and estate planning. The senior coordinator arranges for outside businesses to present educational seminars.

Travel is an important element for seniors in the program. One-day trips are planned to various points of interest. There are even plans to go overseas.

The mature customer is provided a wide range of services, according to Dan Jeff, vice president of marketing. "Banks cannot say they are serving seniors by simply offering them free checking accounts. You must establish a long-term lasting relationship. They tell their friends where they are getting good financial service. In addition, they influence their family members to bank where superior service is provided."

The primary reason for the program's success—they now have 8,000 members—is that the president and chairman of the board made an institutional commitment to the valued senior market. "Our program is not personality-driven as at some banks—if I left, the program would continue," said Jeff.

Family Mutual Bank, Haverhill, Massachusetts

Club Name: Family 55

Requirements: Age 55 or over, $10 per month dues which are waived with combined accounts totaling $25,000

Services: Free NOW account, personalized checks in any style, $10 discount on safe deposit box fees, no-fee traveler's checks, money orders

Other Features: Membership in AARP, $5,000 accidental death insurance, $50,000 common carrier insurance, monthly trips

---

Many banks have a difficult time motivating the front-line personnel to promote the senior program. That situation was resolved at Family Mutual Bank in Haverhill, Massachusetts by including the employees in the travel programs. In fact, places on the overnight trips are so sought after that a lottery system has been instituted.

Linda Steele, marketing assistant, says, "Our staff are effective sales people. They know many of the customers by name and are delighted to promote the senior program to their friends."

Steele feels that the travel aspect as well as the opportunity for socialization is what has caused more than 1,500 seniors to join the program since its inception 18 months ago. Each month a different trip is planned—some are day trips to events and attractions in the Boston area, like the Spirit of Boston trip around Boston Harbor which includes a lobster and clambake bash. Other trips include three-day, two-night theater trips to New York City, a five-day trip to Bermuda, New Year's Eve in Montreal, foliage trips to Mt. Washington in September and more. The only month in which the group does not plan a trip is February.

Each of the trips is preceded by a social hour in the bank's main branch lobby. Refreshments consist of mimosas, sandwiches, soft drinks, coffee, etc. This provides a relaxed social hour which the seniors look forward to as much as the trips.

The buses that transport members on longer trips are equipped with VCRs to show movies out and back. In addition, the escorts serve refreshments. The cost of the trips to the members of Family 55 is minimal—just enough to cover costs including two bank employees who go along on each bus as escorts. Sometimes one of the escorts is a bank senior officer—even the president of the bank has gone along—which has been a good learning experience for senior management.

The year-long schedule of trips is promoted only internally and by a listing in social and senior sections of local newspapers and other senior publications. When the initial mailing was sent to customers describing the club and offering the Spirit of Boston trip for $25, it was timed to arrive the day before Social Security checks were due to be deposited—a

Wednesday when the bank is only open half a day. Thursday morning the customers were lining up before the bank opened and by noon all 120 tickets had been sold with a waiting list of 180 more! An additional trip was planned to accommodate all those who wanted to go. The same trip had been offered by the local senior center, but the bank customers who signed up said they preferred the bank trip so they wouldn't be with "all those old people." Bank trips are considered upscale.

The average combined balance of Family 55 members is $74,000. Members are charged a $10 membership fee per month unless they maintain a minimum balance of $25,000 in combined accounts. Most of the members range in age from 55 to 65 instead of being older retirees. According to Steele, one of the reasons to schedule the programs a year in advance is so that those members still working can schedule their vacations around the trips.

1st National Bank, Grand Forks, North Dakota

Club Name: 55 and Better

Program Launch: November, 1987

Requirements: Age 55 and over, $100 minimum balance in checking account

Services: Free checking, $5 off rental of a safe deposit box, free checks and one free session with a certified financial planner

1st National Bank in Grand Forks did extensive market research before offering its customers 55 and over a membership program. According to Peggy Mastel, marketing officer, the bank's trading area had a great concentration of retired, affluent customers. Rival Metropolitan Savings and Loan started Metro Club, which offered customers free checks and chartered trips at discounted rates. "We really felt committed to providing our customers with a more comprehensive package of services," said Mastel.

Since the program was launched in November, 1987, $4,779,000 has been brought in and deposited to the 55 and Better club, which signed up 1,625 members. The new accounts of new money come from 13 percent of the total membership thus far.

Mastel feels the program has been extremely successful. "Not only has it brought in significant deposits, but we were also able to generate $1.1 million in new loans to members who wanted to buy a condo, townhouse or lake home. Many of our members are snow birds who bought a second or third home in Arizona, Texas or Florida," said Mastel. The average loan was $60,000.

1st National subscribes to FISI Services. A decision was made to contract with FISI after determining that the bank did not have the staff resources or time to manage all the non-financial services. According to the three-year contract FISI agreed not to provide the same package of services to any financial institution within a 100-mile radius.

The advertising budget spent from November 1987 to October 1988 was $30,000 or 10% of the total marketing budget. The bank used newspaper advertising and direct mail to promote the program benefits. It also provided information for inclusion in several senior citizen newsletters.

Mastel feels they have learned a lot in the last year. She feels they tremendously underestimated the amount of staff commitment that was necessary to keep the program going and growing. They also found lower usage than expected from some services.

Mastel said that members did not feel comfortable calling an 800 number to make travel arrangements. In addition, several local travel agencies that were bank customers became upset when the bank elected to use a service outside the state. The bank also found that members were not taking advantage of the discount pharmacy service; once again, they preferred dealing with their local drug store. Mastel indicated that the local pharmacies also were unhappy that the bank was promoting a service outside the state.

As the program was evaluated by top management, Mastel said they had to scramble to put together a report on the results, but top management has agreed to continue the program. In addition, 55 and Better will now have a full-time coordinator who will be responsible for the program.

Farmers & Mechanics Savings Bank, Middleton, Connecticut

Club Name: The Richer Life

Program Launch: October 7, 1988

Requirements: Age 50 or older, $20,000 on deposit in a variety of accounts as long as it includes a NOW or checking account

Services: Special certificates of deposit including six-month and one-year CDs, ATM card, free checks, free money orders

Other Features: Quarterly newsletter, seminars, coordinated group trips, and membership in AARP

Farmers & Mechanics Savings Bank subscribed to the Richer Life, a turn-key program, for two reasons: 1) to prevent deposit erosion and 2) to attract new money to the bank.

The program was launched October 7, 1988 and has 1,106 members with an average deposit balance of $81,265. Since the program was introduced the total deposit maintained by members totals $53,310,468. New money recruited as a result of the program's services totals $2,168,165 or about 4 percent of the total.

Len Hippler, the Richer Life coordinator, says, members are always calling for advice on increasing their savings portfolios. They also call to find out information about the next scheduled local trip. Everyone is on a first name basis.

Hippler coordinates the program throughout the 13-branch system. He writes the quarterly newsletter, which contains bank information as well as local and personal news.

They hold seminars for members at least three times a year on such subjects as taxes, investments, probate, trusts, nursing home insurance and senior lifestyles. Speakers with expertise on the topic of interest are recruited from the community.

Travel is a major part of the program for members. Trips are planned long in advance and include: summer theater outings, Newport harbor cruises to see the mansions, trips into New York City to the Culinary Institute, and visits to the Boston Flower Show. In addition, outings are coordinated with other nearby Richer Life programs that include overnight stays in Boston to see a ball game, hear the Boston Pops and attend a reception. Hippler maintains that the bank has no problem getting the 35 people necessary to fill a bus for each planned trip.

An orientation to the Richer Life program was provided to all customer service representatives. They were shown a film called "Aging in America—the Shape of Things to Come," which was produced by Age Wave. All tellers were provided with a thorough orientation on how to sign up members for the program. The teller fills out a membership enrollment form that also serves as the branch tracking report.

To introduce the program, Farmers & Mechanics spent approximately $70,000 using direct mail, billboards, radio and newspaper ads to promote membership benefits.

Farmers & Mechanics finds members are much more loyal to the bank since the program was launched. "We might not always have the most competitive rate, but because of all the extra services we provide members, they are less likely to chase higher rates offered by the competition," says Hippler.

Management Needs to Know the Benefits

Top management must be made aware of the bottom-line importance of the older customer to the bank. According to "Red" Pope, Valley National Bank in Phoenix, Arizona, "The seniors market is viewed by most people in top management as a deposit-only market, and an expensive market for the costly acquisition of those funds. Therefore why work so hard to get the deposits? Management needs to be made aware of the value those deposits have to the bank and how deregulation will continue to increase the competition from insurance companies and brokerage firms that are going after those same dollars."

Pope went on to say that retaining the deposit business is crucial to the bank's overall success. "The older customer cannot be viewed lightly."

Me-Too Membership Programs

The bank that creates and introduces a membership program first in the marketplace will generally have a corner on the seniors market. This will be even more significant if that bank continues to make changes and improvements to the overall program.

The bank that provides a program similar to the one in the market-place will also enjoy favorable returns and results, but the rate of cannibalization will be greater. To avoid this, the bank must be much more inventive and provide unique services not offered by the competition.

As more and more banks make a commitment to capture their share of the mature market customer deposits, there will be a real need to be unique. Differentiation will be the key. As it is now, senior membership programs are virtually identical coast-to-coast. The bank about to enter the mature marketplace has a real challenge to be distinctive. That will be a constant challenge, because it will be the truly "special" program that will attract the coming baby boom depositors.

Our Recommendations

☐ Be sure to make a commitment to support the member program with adequate staff to ensure the program's success.

☐ It is absolutely essential that top management make the commitment to older customers a top priority. The program cannot succeed without that commitment.

☐ Stay current; be aware of changing trends and demographic shifts. Each group approaching 50 brings with it a new set of spending and savings needs.

☐ Network with mature market specialists outside the banking circles. Avoid making decisions based on what the bank down the street is doing.

☐ Be distinct and unique with the program of services—remember to improve and enhance existing programs. Bring in an outside consultant to objectively evaluate and audit the program if necessary.

☐ Determine what business you want to be in—don't provide travel or pharmacy services if the customers don't use them.

☐ Give careful thought to the advantages and disadvantages of using turn-key providers. Whatever the decision, it requires a commitment of both staff and top management.

☐ Provide adequate training and orientation to customer contact people and top management. Provide the people signing up customers with an incentive.

☐ Don't build up a head of steam for a one-year only program. Plan to make a long-term commitment to this dynamic market.

☐ Reach outside the bank to get involved in the community, senior centers, continuing care facilities, hospitals, malls, hotels, and department stores to create a sense of involvement.

6 Pre-Retirement Seminars and Social Activities

Common Mistakes

1 Failure to realize that the social nature of mature customers is the cornerstone for building customer loyalty.

2 Lack of understanding about how the older customer responds to civic and community activities.

3 Failure to link the bank's corporate giving and community sponsorships to the mature market.

4 Senior management not permitting the bank to sponsor trips, tours, excursions, cruises and parties when they prove to be the glue that holds a program together.

5 Turning arrangements for travel over to a travel agency ill-equipped to deal with the physical and psychological needs of older customers.

6 Failure to take advantage of opportunities provided by pre-retirement training seminars

W hy do group social events like travel programs or trips sponsored by the bank, educational activities such as financial planning seminars, and participation in fitness programs such as the Senior Olympics have special appeal to the seniors market? And, more important to bankers, what business value is there in developing programs like these?

The answer to these questions are based on the attitudes, beliefs, feelings and values of the older person.

Clearly, the older person is in a different place attitudinally than the younger person and in a different stage in the life cycle. Most of today's older Americans have lived through the first of life's acquisitive stages, purchasing products to support their needs first as single consumers, then often as parents, to support the needs of their developing families. As they age, their interest in products becomes less important to them. They become more concerned with what is known as "life satisfaction."

They want a sense of pleasure in life's activities, a feeling that they are achieving their goals. They want to lead a meaningful life, to feel optimistic about what the world has to offer.[1]

62

The result of these concerns for those charged with marketing responsibilities is that the old rules of product and service satisfaction are no longer applicable. In its place, new initiatives and approaches must be used to reach the growing mature market. The new initiative for the financial services marketer is creating a sense of belonging for that sector of the customer base to which it is significant.

As an example, instead of marketing retirement housing as an attractive arrangement of living space with meals and other services provided, we market the facility in terms of the satisfying experiences which it will afford the buyer—time spent with friends, shared experiences and opportunities for growth.

And when marketing continuing education courses for the elderly, we don't talk about the information that will be imparted but about the feelings of satisfaction which will stem from remaining involved with the world around us.[2]

The Mature Market Seminar

The mature consumer can learn about lifestyle planning, pre-retirement and personal development ideas through many sources including books, print and broadcast media, and individual experiences. One of the best ways to draw on each of these learning modes is through a mature market seminar or related program sponsored by the financial institution.

With any subject matter, people can help other people through the free exchange of experiences, insights, ideas and opinions. Though seminars can be conducted under several formats, their success is based on the fact that mature adults have a wealth of experience to draw on. They look for practical answers and case studies that show how others solved a problem. They view themselves as needing continuing education for the future.

When a financial institution sponsors such an outing or a lecture it shows the mature customer a concern about such issues that goes beyond the personal finance area. It also reinforces the bank as knowledgeable about issues facing the mature market and as an important planning source.

Most Pressing Need for Information

Pre-retirement training was noted as the most pressing need of nearly 70 percent of the people responding to a survey in a "Retired in America" study by the Retirement Advisors Division of Hearst Business Communications. The study of retired people who were receiving private pensions and/or profit sharing was a 1988 update of the benchmark study the firm did in 1984. The results provide fertile ground for those banks actively involved in providing seminars, workshops, social events and other group functions. The results of the survey are reported in Chapter 1.

This research paints a picture of a healthy, well-off retiree interested in doing things that are rewarding, not interested in working but being involved in worthwhile activities. Pre-retirement training is a perfect opportunity for a bank to solidify relationships with the older customer, provide meaningful information that the retiree wants and build a bridge to a stronger customer relationship.

Competitive Situation

When planning, organizing and promoting pre-retirement seminars or workshops, it is important for the bank marketer to know of similar programs in the area. Often, mature market classes and topics are covered at local hospitals, YMCAs, professional organizations and continuing education programs at universities. Many of the women's service hospitals, which offer diagnostic and educational counseling programs to women, have developed extensive educational bills of fare covering topics from osteoporosis to overcoming grief after a death in the family.

Choosing a Format

The number of participants, background of the program leader and budget constraints will help determine the most appropriate format. Certainly, any combination of the meetings can be combined in a program series. The basic formats for a mature market planning and discussion series are as follows.

- Lecture: This format entails a 20-30 minute presentation by an expert followed by a question and answer period. The major benefit of this format lies in its adaptability. The number of participants is unlimited. The program administrator can rely on the expert speaker for program material since there is little interaction other than the Q & A.

- Lecture/workshop: This format enhances the basic lecture or address by adding one or more elements to increase participation by the attendees. Following the presentation, a buzz session, quiz, brainstorming session, discussion, or break-to-groups is held. An unlimited number of participants can be involved. The planner must ensure that the participatory section runs smoothly.

- Seminar: The seminar is a small group discussion. After an initial presentation of some type to initiate discussion, the attendees in effect become the experts on the subject. Conversation revolves around past experiences and personal opinions on a subject of interest to all. The group can range in size from 10 to 25.

The seminar or lecture series is a fundamental part of the complete mature marketing program. The target audience for such educational offerings is the same as for the overall program. The planning and promotion of these events should be focused on this group. It is important not to limit any of the programs by age requirements. Any member of the family—sons, daughters, other close family members—who has an interest in such topics will provide an interesting perspective for participants.

Much of the pre-retirement or lifestyle planning involves important family decisions. Planning in this regard by only one partner could lead to family friction or unhappiness. The host organization should select dates, times and places that allow couples to attend together. By mixing the dates and times to include both morning and evening sessions, more mature customers will attend the event. Unmarried participants should be encouraged to bring a close relative or friend. If possible, hold the events at the member institution to maximize the relationship with the host in the eyes of the attendees. Discussion with a few prospective attendees can help the administrator in site selection and finding the best date and time.

When using handouts, workbooks and other take-home materials, it's important to maintain appeal for a wide audience. Blue-collar workers, clerical employees, retirees, middle-management personnel and top executives will sit side-by-side at such an event. Much of the existing literature on mature issues is written for wide appeal.

Who Shifts the Gears?

The majority of the mature market educational programs will be conducted by a discussion leader and a resource authority. Each program can be different but these two members of the "seminar faculty" can adequately manage the necessary program elements for a lively discussion or lecture.

Discussion leader: The key to a successful program, the discussion leader acts as the administrator for the entire program. Knowledge of the subject is not the most important factor for the discussion leader. This person's responsibilities include moving the program along smoothly, making deadlines, encouraging group discussion and directing questions to the appropriate speaker, attendee or resource material. It is vital that the discussion leader facilitate or lead the discussion to bring out different aspects of the issue. Expert facilitating takes practice. It means not interjecting opinions or evaluating comments made by others. As a moderator, the discussion leader asks questions that require more than a yes or no answer.

Resource authority: The resource authority must concentrate on research and practical application of the various subjects that will make up the program calendar. The resource authority must provide the attendees with a human resource for important statistics, case studies and details about trends within the national mature consumer community.

Certified financial planners, tax experts and others associated with the bank or with professional services like CPA or tax law firms can conduct the sessions. Take care to check these people out beforehand for their ability to present and relate to the audience.

Managing the Educational Event

A good lecture/workshop will motivate participants to openly discuss and analyze the topic at hand. The attendees will recognize a well-managed seminar and the work of a prepared discussion leader and resource authority. The easiest way to encourage participation is to earmark a section for just that purpose. Every effort should be made to offer the lecture/workshop rather than a straight lecture program. Three factors predispose the mature market customer to get involved in a lecture format:

1. These adults gravitate toward doing rather than merely listening.
2. They enjoy relating new information to real life experiences and life situations.
3. Exchanging ideas with others in a similar situation with similar concerns is very important to this group.

Leading large groups in thoughtful discussion to achieve solutions takes practice and skill. These general rules can help move such programs along smoothly and garner results from participants:

■ Give clear and complete instructions. Provide typed handouts describing the directions, problem or assignments. An agenda for the entire program will help participants follow along and will help the leader time the presentations.

■ Offer comfortable and attractive physical arrangements. If a great deal of writing will take place, have desks or clipboards and writing materials. Give attendees enough time between sessions to move from buzz groups to and from reporting sessions. Use frequent breaks especially if there are lengthy sit-down sessions.

■ Have a microphone on stage or at an elevated platform so that large groups can hear the lecture. If necessary, have the speaker repeat questions.

■ Orient the lecturer or resource authority so that he or she fully understands the goals and timing of the program. The lecturer should feel free to move around and listen in on the buzz sessions or make contributions to the brainstorming.

As the coordinator gains experience with the different formats it is possible to experiment with the various techniques and combinations of techniques to maximize participant involvement and results.

The question and answer period is part of the lecture format. At the outset, designate a specific time to answer questions. Without a preordained Q & A section, the presentation is subject to interruptions or having the program run too long. Make sure everyone can hear the questions. Repeat then if necessary. Have two or three questions ready to "prime the pump."

Ask participants who have very personal questions to ask them after the program or discuss them with personal advisors.

Sample Topics

When wading through the wealth of potential topics, it's important for the coordinator to consider both input from potential attendees and programs that have been covered at area community colleges, civic groups, churches and hospitals. To aid in planning these seminars, here are some examples of interesting topics with the mature market in mind:

Retirement Employment

Where Will You Live?

Sources of Income

Relationships

Coping with Stress

Wellness and Nutrition

Investment Strategies

Legal Affairs and Estate Planning

Your Role in the Family

The Empty Nest Years

Time: Friend or Foe?

Relocation

Housing Needs and Options

Sports and Fitness

Dealing with a Death in the Family

Personal Financial Planning

Area Transportation

So You'd Like to Travel

Your New Roles—At Home and in the Community

Starting from Scratch: New Hobbies

New Free Time; New Interests

Sponsoring Existing Senior Programs

The two primary concerns of people over 50 are that they will out-live their financial nest egg and that their health will deteriorate and cause them to become dependent on someone else for their care.

Surveys have shown that 94 percent of the over-50 market is mobile and active; 80 percent live independently and want to remain that way for as long as possible.

In fact, most seem to have adopted the philosophy of the vigorous French cellist, Paul Tortellier, who said on his seventieth birthday: "Every-one should aim to die young, but delay doing so for as long as possible."

George Burns describes a common problem of aging in his best seller, *How to Live to be 100 or More,* this way, "To me, the greatest danger of retirement is what it can do to your attitude. When you have all that time on your hands, you think old, you act old. I've seen people who, the minute they turn 65, start rehearsing to be old. They start taking little steps. They practice grunting when they sit down and when they get up. They take little naps when you're talking to them and by the time they get to be 70 they've made it—a hit—they're now old. Not me!"

Robert H. Butler, M.D. Director of the National Institute on Aging said, "If exercise could be packed into a pill, it would be the single most widely prescribed and beneficial medicine in the nation."

Banks that are actively targeting seniors would benefit by sponsor-ing events and programs that are geared to helping them stay not only financially but physically fit.

Association and identification with events and programs geared to making seniors aware of their health options would contribute to the bank's positive image among households in this older segment.

Potential Opportunities

Senior Expos—Senior Fairs can be an effective way to get your mes-sage to the targeted older customer. Well-organized Senior Fairs in Min-neapolis, Albuquerque, Los Angeles, New York, Portland and Seattle provide many opportunities to get much needed financial planning information into the hands of interested seniors.

"Senior Options" Expo is a nationally recognized, award-winning, two-day lifestyle and resource exposition. It showcases the multitude of options available to help the mature market stay active, healthy and inde-pendent. The four-year-old Minneapolis/St. Paul "Senior Options" Expo draws more than 10,000 seniors. The first Duluth, Minnesota, "Senior Options" Expo drew 6,000 participants. As a result of the successful record, a non-profit joint venture has been established called "Senior Options USA" (SOUSA) which helps other communities develop Senior Expos in their area. First Bank System in Minneapolis was a major spon-sor of the 1988 "Senior Options" Expo.

First Bank System sponsored the "Walk of Ages" and its Grand Marshal was Alice Faye. The walk, a first-time event, was a non-competitive, one-mile jaunt for people of all ages. The bank also offered participants at the Senior Options Expo four seminars on personal finance.

In addition, First Bank System was an exhibitor at the Expo. According to Julie Schultz Brown, vice president at First Bank System, "The Expo was a wonderful well-attended event for us to be a part of. It gave us a unique opportunity to reach a lot of seniors in one place at one time."

The "Senior Options" Expo was such a success for First Bank System that plans are already in the works to include it in 1989.

State Senior Olympic Games—Approximately 500,000 seniors age 55 and over compete in feeder Games in their states in hopes of qualifying for the U.S. National Senior Olympic Games.

The events include track and field, swimming, tennis, volleyball, shuffleboard, badminton, archery, horseshoes, golf, a 10K road race, cycling and softball.

Lisa Auswald, vice president of community affairs at People's Bank in Bridgeport, Connecticut, finds the event a very positive, upbeat way to reach potential bank customers. During the 1988 Games, People's Bank supplied 3,000 T-shirts to the athletes and spectators. In addition, People's used the opportunity to distribute literature about the bank's services. In the Games, People's Bank plans to use the sporting event as a means to promote health and fitness as they launch a more aggressive program to reach older bank customers.

NCNB in Charlotte, North Carolina, also gets very involved as a sponsor of the event as a community relations vehicle. The North Carolina Games have over 5,000 participants. The Games attract the media attention of local TV shows, newspapers and senior publications.

Barnett Banks in Jacksonville, Florida, encourages its bank branches to sponsor the local Senior Olympics. The Games provide a great deal of visibility for local branches.

Senior Olympics events are much more than a sporting event; they are also a social event, a family affair, and an inspiration for all those involved. The event provides the sponsorship opportunities to reach families of seniors, their children and grandchildren and the spectators who take pride in the achievements of people their own age. Sponsorship of Senior Olympics offers a unique intergenerational promotional opportunity for banks to reach the viable active market segment in a positive fashion.

Blood pressure, glaucoma and fitness tests at malls, branches and local Y's—Linda Sudendorf, director of marketing at Skokie Federal Savings in Skokie, Illinois, finds this service generates a large turn-out. Skokie Federal sponsors health screenings regularly at branch offices and more than 300 people participate in a six-hour period. Skokie's 12-year-old senior program reaches 50,000 loyal, mature customers.

Health walks at local enclosed malls—Every morning at shopping malls across the country seniors can be found walking in the malls for a variety of reasons. Some people walk as a result of doctor's orders; others do so for the social aspect of walking and the more serious walkers do so because it is their primary form of exercise.

A bank could explore premiums and new incentives, such as providing discounts on walking shoes. Sweatsuits with the bank's name imprinted on them would be like having walking billboards at the malls.

Events at the local bowling alley—According to the National Bowling Council (NBC) there are over 6.2 million senior people who bowl. Bowling centers are always interested in filling up the lanes during non-peak, off hours with bowling for seniors.

Older people bowl for a variety of reasons: Nearly all join for companionship, 92 percent because they want to be part of a team and 66 percent for the exercise, according to NBC statistics. Banks could sponsor a Senior League Tournament or other competitive event. In 1988, 49 states held senior tournaments which attracted thousands of participants. In addition, the Professional Bowlers Association has a seniors tournament every year.

Available Masters and Seniors Sports Events—The Masters Swimming, Track and Field, Tennis and Distance Running are unique because they offer an intergenerational spirit of healthy competition. These events give men and women past their 20s and 30s a second chance at winning medals.

They provide a year-round schedule of meets and tournaments that offers participants an expanded social circle and provides a reason to travel worldwide.

The U.S.T.A. Seniors Tennis is designed for players 35 and up. Interested banks could sponsor or organize a "recreational doubles" tournament. Send for a starter kit ($10 from U.S.T.A. Publications, 729 Alexander Road, Princeton, NJ 08540). The kit provides certificates for winners and a poster to get interest going and encourage participation.

Masters Distance Running and Track and Field programs are for runners over 35. Competition is segmented by age from 40 to 85 in five year increments. There are 25,000 active runners who participate in running and walking events like the 5K, 8K, 10K, 20K, 30K, 50K, 50 miles and 100 miles. Contact The Athletics Congress, P.O. Box 120, Indianapolis, IN 46206 (317) 636-9155.

U.S. Masters Swimming program is for swimmers aged 25 to 92. About 10,000 to 12,000 members in individual and team formats participate in the hundreds of local, state, regional, zone and national events. The U.S.M.S. meets are as much for social get-togethers as they are for serious competition among athletes. There are 56 chapters throughout the country. For information, contact: Dot Donnelly, 5 Piggot Lane, Avon, CT 06001.

Bank-Created Events

There are many tours, trips and social events that can be sponsored by banks. Often there are local sources for conducting these events. The following is a list of social activities developed by a number of banks:

- First Valley Bank in Bethlehem, Pennsylvania, formed its First Valley Club with the sponsorship of the Senior Citizens Center of Bethlehem. The bank plans trips to fairs and museums, sports and cultural events, tours of historic shrines, and day trips to the Pocono Mountains and New Jersey seashore. The bank also holds an annual picnic, square dances, bingo nights and a Club dinner each fall.

- Sentry Bank in Orleans, Massachusetts, sponsored a senior citizens' exposition including a luncheon and workshops on health, housing and financial subjects.

- The Eagle River State Bank in Eagle River, Wisconsin, sponsors a Senior Prom for its seniors club, the Golden Eagles Club, and chooses a king and queen.

- Unifirst Bank for Savings, Jackson, Mississippi, held a Christmas party for its Prime of Life Club members. More than 2,000 Club members attended the Club's Christmas party.

- Commerce Bank & Trust, Topeka, Kansas, has Christmas light tours, dinner theater, baseball game trips and bus trips to New York City's Macy's parade.

Our Recommendations

☐ The bank should develop a series of educational sessions on pre-retirement planning, using the bank's own people or others who have been retained to do the sessions.

☐ Working with capable sources, the bank should look to provide special social events with older customers. These could be held in the bank lobby, at a nearby hotel or in the bank's conference or civic room.

☐ Set up an advisory board of seniors to work with the bank on understanding the needs of the mature customers and how the bank can hold bank-centered activities that support customers.

☐ Follow up on all activities of a social and educational nature. Many an excellent program is run and attended by many customers but the bank is not able to respond in some way.

Notes
1. George Miaoulis, Ph.D., and Phillip Cooper, Ph. D., "The Satisfaction Syndrome," *Marketing Communications,* March, 1987, P. 36.
2. Op. cit. P. 37.

7 Communicating with the Mature Market

Common Mistakes

1 Lack of understanding of generational differences, especially in communicating with the mature market.

2 Using words, images, labels and concepts in communicating with the seniors market that are considered demeaning or patronizing by the older person.

3 Failure to understand that the elderly customer is an avid reader of articles, advertisements and direct mail copy.

4 Lack of understanding of the learning deficiencies, as well as declining sight, hearing, touch and strength of the older consumer.

5 Assuming that the older consumer responds to advertising the same way other segments do.

6 Failure to understand that the mature person responds favorably to bank communication that explains and unfavorably to communication that sells.

The greatest ongoing challenge to bankers in building or maintaining a relationship with older customers and the mature market is in communicating effectively. While the subject of communications may deal with a number of forms—oral, written, visual, expressed and implied—this chapter deals with communication media that the bank marketer controls or influences. These media include print and broadcast advertising, newsletters, the telephone and brochures. (Interpersonal communication is covered in Chapter 10.)

The Copy Platform

Developing precise advertising communications that stress the rational benefits of the product is important. Older consumers are not averse to trying new things. There is a strongly held belief that once an individual gets to a certain age he or she will not change. Specialists in mature marketing have found this definitely not to be true. Seniors are not set in their ways; certainly not in terms of the consumer products they buy. They want to be open to what is going on and be able to make decisions about new products and services being offered to consumers.

They will try new products, compare them and decide whether they fit their needs. Financial services marketers should not automatically

73

conclude that those over age 50 will not be interested in a savings, investment and credit product which is tailored to the younger segment.

This age group enjoys honest, true to life and genuine portrayals of children on television commercials because it is a reminder of a happy childhood, says Susan Wirtzel.[1] Children also reinforce the value seniors place on family, which they consider the basis of life. They like to see romance and portrayals that idealize life and relationships. This appeal validates their feelings that people aren't forgotten in today's rush to sell products and services, she adds.

They like real-life situations with happy endings and resolutions that reinforce something they believe in. Story advertising provides them with escapism and a vicarious experience. Seniors like to see celebrities being themselves on camera and endorsing products they really use and know about. They feel that celebrities of their day are part of their world, their past, their values and the role they've played in the development of our society.

Sources of Information for Buying Choices

Because the elderly market has not been given serious consideration by many companies until recently, the body of research about this unique market is limited. One subject which has received minimal study but which has value to bank marketers in developing advertising plans is an identification of the sources of information used by the older consumer in making decisions to purchase products and services.

In a research study conducted for the AARP-Andrus Foundation, two professors sampled a group of affluent, better educated elderly and non-elderly consumers.[2] The research results identified a tendency by the elderly, in contrast to the non-elderly, to rely more heavily on advertiser-supplied information when forming price/quality evaluations.

As part of the explanation, researchers concluded that the elderly typically are under limitations in their mobility and in their sphere of influence and thus are forced to use more sources of information. Because of the reduced income levels at which many of them live, they need to be aware of more options. They view information provided by advertisers more favorably than other age segments.

The findings suggest to advertisers the potential opportunity to establish a more favorable position for products among the older customer through the use of product-related information, prior to and at the point of sale. Information may be communicated through various sources, such as catalogs, trade publications, and point-of purchase promotions. Information should be presented in a way that makes it easy to make a price/quality evaluation and purchase decision.

Both older and younger consumer groups place the greatest emphasis on guarantees, product and store reputation and personal evaluations. Compared with the non-elderly consumer, the elderly do not rely more

heavily on their own experiences or that of "significant others" for pur-
chase-related information. While rated lower in overall importance, older
customers rely more heavily on sales people and independent sources for
information compared with their younger counterparts.

Further, the report stated that retail entities who respond to the
elderly's need in an expedient manner are well received. Mature consumers would pay more to shop in a store that went after the business of
retirement-aged people. Other research has shown that a substantial
percentage of older consumers want store personnel to treat older consumers with more courtesy, dignity and patience. Most older consumers
are dissatisfied with their treatment, and they perceive lack of interest,
impatience and rudeness on the part of the store employees.

Learning Deficiencies with Older Consumers

A significant difference between the older and the younger person
is the ability to process information. This applies more to seniors over 65
years old and it has an impact on the effectiveness of advertising directed
to them.

The elderly clearly have a general learning deficiency.[3] They consistently perform at a lower level in memory tests at all learning levels.
The source of this learning deficit is associated with the encoding stage
of information processing—the point at which information is placed in
memory. Both aided and recognition recall and unaided recall indicate
memory deficiencies.

This study states that the older person consistently learns less than
younger adults and the level of the learning decrement increases under
certain conditions. Showing a print ad to a younger adult increases memory performance but does not have the same memory recall effect with
an older person.

The study also suggests that the elderly have encoding deficiencies
when processing information from print or television advertisements.
They may not benefit from promotional efforts to increase recognition,
and therefore point-of-purchase displays do not seem to be useful as
promotional devices to supplement advertising information.

Another study suggests that decreases in learning and processing of
information can be compensated for by increasing the older consumer's
familiarity with the task by keeping messages simple and to the point, or
by increasing the frequency of the message.[4]

The older person's susceptibility to persuasion is specific to the
situation. When the elderly perceive themselves to be competent, they
appear to be no more susceptible to social influences than younger
adults. The implication is that a variety of messages and appeals may be
appropriate for banking products and services aimed at sub-segments of
the elderly population.

75

A SRI report on business opportunities with the aging states that older people have fewer problems recalling recently acquired information which is presented in a simple, straightforward way.[5] On the other hand, problems occur when irrelevant, distracting information follows the information to be remembered.

Without interference, older persons recall and remember as well as younger adults on short-term memory tasks, such as remembering a list or a phone number, when the length of the information is about seven numbers or three to four words. One difference: older persons can recognize better than they can recall freely. Thus they can identify names and numbers on sight better than they can recall them without clues.

Older persons become aware of the limits of advancing age and attempt to compensate for them in different ways. They clearly recognize the necessity of taking advice. They compensate in other ways by conserving time and resources, particularly their energy, and differentiating between what is necessary and what is unnecessary among their demands. They tend to exploit their intellectual resources more fully than do others. They have a subtle perception of the places where the complexity of their decisions exceeds their capacity.

Portraying Older Persons in Bank Advertising

A primary consideration in marketing to the mature customer, as we have stated earlier, is that older consumers think of themselves not at their current age level but 7 to 10 years younger. What does that mean when using photographs of individuals in this market? Many marketers agree, a middle-of-the-road approach is called for. Using models who are neither too old nor too young is appropriate. Also include pictures of representative single, active women, an important segment in the mature market.

There is a general feeling that older consumers, except for the affluent, care only about cost savings and inexpensive products.

Research does not bear that out. Older models used in advertisements are not exclusively associated with less expensive product classes or with health, hygiene or household products.[6]

Table 1 shows how the use of elderly individuals in advertising varies by product class. The results of the study proved to be interesting because the advertisement categories with a high percentage of elderly people were generally of expensive products with some upscale appeal.

Table 1-Use of Elderly in Ads by Product Class

Product Class	Percent of Ads Portraying Elderly
Liquor	20.9
Cars and Trucks	17.2
Banks	17.2
Cameras	16.4
Magazines and Newspapers	16.4
Electronics and Communications	15.2
Hotels	14.3
Music	14.3
Institutional	14.1
Jewelry	13.5
Machinery	13.5
Sporting Goods	13.0
Travel and Vacations	12.5
Health and Medicine	10.8
Society (charities, etc.)	9.0
Food	7.3
Hygiene (diet aids, shampoo)	6.5
Tobacco	6.3
Household (appliances, tools, etc.)	4.1
Clothing	2.7
Cosmetics	0.7

Source: Anthony C. Ursic, Michael L. Ursic, Virginia L. Ursic, "A Longitudinal Study of the Use of the Elderly in Magazine Advertising," Journal of Consumer Research, June, 1986, P. 131.

The People's Choice: Print Media

Those 65 and older read and watch more news than the average consumer. They read more local newspapers and watch more television. They tend to turn to the print media for information and to the broadcast media for entertainment.

As the marketing director of the "New Age" program of Donnelley Marketing, a division of the Dun & Bradstreet corporation, puts it, "You can reach this audience very effectively through print media because they are active information seekers who tend to read significantly more than any other segment of the population."[7]

Because they are such prolific readers, older consumers' approach to the printed word is different from that of other segments. For example, they are very much interested in obtaining information from the media, not just being entertained by it. They read newspaper ads as well as direct mail pieces carefully. In many ways they look at advertisements as a way to help them develop and prepare shopping lists. Notice how well organized an older person generally is when he or she arrives at the supermarket. Frequently they shop with a list in hand and a handful of coupons they have collected.

Since they rely on printed matter as a primary means of generating opinions and they may have physical impairments such as vision difficulties, marketers who develop printed matter for this market should understand that often they can be confused by too much irrelevant information. They tend to process information more slowly. With cues to remember past ads, these marketers will be more successful in their promotional strategy.

Adds John Migliacio of Retirement Advisers, a division of Hearst Business Communications, Inc., New York:[8] Make print, not waves. Print is the preferred medium among seniors to get information. They want something they can carry away and study. They are magazine, newspaper, letter and booklet readers who want written materials that boil down information and present it clearly and keep it simple.

You can never tell older customers enough. If you use short ad copy, be sure to follow up with more information. Consider giving away things like informational materials, how-to guides and personal aids. Don't forget to thank seniors who have been long-term customers.

R. J. Balkite, marketing manager for Donnelley Marketing, has developed this list of guidelines for developing print advertisements:[9]

- Forget the term "senior citizen." Don't refer to consumers in the 50-plus category as senior citizens. If you must single out this group, use "mature Americans." As a rule, however, try to avoid any direct reference to age.

- Clarity is the key. Your text should be clear, easy-to-read, personalized and involve the reader. Keep paragraphs brief and concise. Type should be large enough to be read easily. Avoid small, excessively large or ornate typefaces in print ads.

- Shop-by-mail offers are attractive. Older consumers are, on average, twice as likely as U.S. consumers in general to buy products by mail. The age 50-plus consumer is also significantly more responsive to mail promotions, particularly high-value coupons and sampling.

- Use appealing colors. Blues, greens, lavender and pastel shades are favored by this audience. Avoid using browns and grays; they are perceived negatively.

- Use high-value coupons and sampling. Coupons, discounts and incentives appeal to this segment because they reduce risk. These incentives should have 15 to 25 percent greater value than for other segments. Mail-back sampling offers also draw strong responses from consumers age 50 and over. Unconditional warranties, guarantees and comprehensive refund policies are important.

- Testimonials work. Product endorsements by experts such as doctors, pharmacists and other professionals as well as trusted celebrities in the 50-plus age bracket tend to influence this segment.

- Tap research responsiveness. Marketers are likely to get valuable feedback from 50-plus consumers, who are more inclined than other segments to complete questionnaires, participate in surveys or join clubs and associations.

- Use positive lifestyle promotions. This segment responds favorably to ads that depict active men and women together in social situations. Ads depicting a woman alone should portray her as happy and active. Warm scenes—especially those showing individuals touching or holding hands—draw positive responses from this audience.

Finally, Grey Advertising, New York City, provides these tips on marketing to the older consumer:[10]

- Think younger. At least 10 years younger, classic and not trendy, chic not funky, never dowdy.

- Capture their spirit. Depict life as it is for them: desirable, active, sociable, productive and worthy of respect.

- Show togetherness. Nearly 75 percent are living with spouses; show them involved with mates, family friends.

- Make them the stars of the show. Use older persons as spokespersons and role models since they are the voices of authority.

- Tune them in. Use music in ads, but not just golden oldies. Use contemporary artists like Bette Midler, Manhattan Transfer and Linda Ronstadt.

- Remember they are MGM not MTV. Pacing is important in advertising. Steer clear of rapid-fire, unrelated images and quick cuts.

- Treat them like grownups. Give these consumers the facts. They're experienced shoppers and are turned off by hard sell or patronizing ads.

- Put a twinkle in their eyes. Use a little humor in your sales. They are confident enough to laugh at themselves and at life.

- Do not call them names. They hate tags such as senior citizens, mature consumers, golden harvest gang. Don't talk about age. Show how your product meets the needs of the 50-plus age group.

Direct Mail Advertising

The following comments about designing and writing direct mail programs, selecting formats and producing direct mail programs are from an interview with George S. Wachtel, President, WORDCOM, Ellington, Connecticut. WORDCOM is an independent direct mail company, one of the largest in the country specializing in financial services direct marketing. The company serves as the marketing arm for the Richer Life, a firm that supplies a turn-key, packaged program to banks.

Tips for writing copy: Banks tend to describe themselves in terms of why the bank is good and why the bank's products are good instead of what is in it for the consumer—the prime consumer benefit. As people move into their 60s, they tend to have more time and are more inclined to read more copy and visit with the bank personnel on the subject of banking services.

The 35-to-40-year-olds tend to be action-oriented, time-conscious, and when it comes to direct mail, look for ways to reply easily. As a result, they are more willing to act through the mail. The older consumer—age 60-plus—to whom time is not as much a constraint, is anxious to receive the mail each day. It may serve as the highlight of the day and they go to the mailbox in a positive frame of mind. They are looking for good information, and are willing to read longer copy.

With the younger market, a one-page letter is relevant. With seniors, a two page letter is more appropriate, as long as it contains useful, informational copy. Wachtel has found it is far more productive to develop copy that promotes the idea of coming to the bank and getting more information. Direct mail is positioned as an attention-getting, interest-piquing device. With the non-elderly segment and their personal time constraints, selling through the mail is desirable. It is Wachtel's belief that with the seniors market it is best to have them come into the bank for what is called "more conversation."

How to go about it differs from market to market. Often, premiums will work. As its strategy for obtaining new accounts, a $1 billion bank is trading a silver ingot "for a conversation." The bank believes it can convert 25 to 50 percent of all visits into new accounts. The program has a premium with high perceived value and yet a low unit cost, in the $7 range. The target for the campaign is those over age 50 within the state.

Here are points from Wachtel about initiating a direct mail program:

- Begin a program by using the bank's customer base. Some marketers believe this will only cannibalize existing accounts, but Wachtel feels the move will help create loyalty and lock the money into the bank. If the bank does not have age information in its file, usually it has a profile of customers by product category. Selections can be made on deposit levels, mortgage balances or discount brokerage usage.

- Buy a mailing list from a commercial list house, selecting prospects by age and income. Age information is available from list houses that compile lists from voter and automobile registrations.

■ Three factors are important in list selection. The first is geographical—is this the true market to be served by the bank? Bank products like credit cards and home equity lines of credit can be sold across state lines, but this is unlikely for a seniors program especially if the strategy is positioned for the customer to visit the bank. Second is the age requirement—usually seeking households with at least one senior in them. Third is income. This should reflect the market and the level should be raised for those locations that have higher wages, standards of living and level of affluence.

Realize that any list purchased from a commercial supplier will have a number of deceased persons on it. Those include both persons who have died since the list was compiled and those who have been deliberately left on the list, e.g., a widow leaves her deceased spouse as the listing in the phone book for personal security reasons. The upshot will be that a number of letters will arrive at the bank from people who write that their spouse passed away many years ago and are unaware that the list came from the telephone directory.

According to Wachtel, given seniors' available time and interest in the printed word, targeting direct mail can prove to be a highly successful method of reaching this audience. Using the right list, complete information and a tantalizing offer can bring deposit results.

Print Advertising—Newspapers

Among the growing number of options available to the bank seeking the most efficient way of reaching the mature market on a localized basis is the Seniors Publishing Group, San Diego. The firm is a national and regional advertising rep firm representing 95 newspapers across the United States. Regional and other multistate banks might look at this as an opportunity to reach the seniors market.

The company represents a number of monthly mature market publications with a combined circulation of close to four million, according to Leonard Hansen, chairman. The firm provides a single-contract, single-invoice service with a sales representative handling all the papers.

The firm offers national advertisers the local commissionable rate on all buys. This is the same rate a local financial services institution receives. Among the national advertisers are Greyhound, United, TWA, Holiday Inns, Embassy Suites and Mutual of Omaha.

Print Media—Magazines

The market for national mature magazines has grown in recent years. Among the better known are *Modern Maturity,* a bimonthly publication of the American Association of Retired Persons; monthly *New Choices,* Retirement Living Publishing Company, a Reader's Digest company; *Lear's,* a bimonthly publication for the mature woman, and *Golden Years,* a monthly from the Seniors Services Group.

81

Among the others finding a unique way to attract mature market readers is McCall's. It has added a bimonthly insert to create a "demographic edition" for the more than a million subscribers in the 50 to 60 age segment. The "Silver Edition," as it is called, contains features on travel, financial planning, leisure and health.

The Appendix lists additional information about publications for the mature market.

Electronic Media

Advertisers and advertising agencies must break out of the rut if they plan to market their services to the mature market.[11] They need to place more value on the electronic media—network TV, cable, radio and the VCR. Usually when a media plan is created, it is structured in terms of quantitative measurement and the lowest cost per thousand. Contemporary thinking is to make two traditional age group buys—men and women 18 to 49 and men and women age 25 to 54.

Pricing is set by the media exclusively in these norms. The electronic media seldom track the senior market listeners or viewers. This occurs in spite of the growing body of research emphasizing changing lifestyles and increasing discretionary buying power. National electronic media should understand that the emphasis needs to be placed on the value of changing the demographics to include the 35-64 segment to insure the advertiser a balanced buy.

Radio Advertising

The electronic medium that has been most responsive to the changes in demographic trends is the radio industry. The Radio Advertising Bureau has provided the media buying community with data about the advantages of making a 35-64 age group demographics buy over the traditional age 25 to 54 demographics.

Within the advertising industry, The 35 Plus Committee has been formed to develop an informational campaign targeted to erasing the mindset that it believes advertisers and advertising agencies have about the 50-plus market. The committee, which formerly was called the 35 to 64 Committee, changed its name because it realized the numbers of the age groups it was focusing on was extending to age 70.

The committee offers a 16-minute, large screen presentation called "The Amazing Invisible Market," using the comedy team of Stiller and Meara as narrators, to be shown in a number of markets around the country. According to chairman Maurice Webster, "They are done with teething, past the PTA and all that. They're enjoying life. People who used to depend on their children to help them through their silver years are living by themselves. They have the income to do what they like and they are doing it."[12]

Advertising to reach the mature market via radio has not proven to be effective. While radio station management is aware of the demographics of the mature market, especially the coming impact of the baby boomers, there have been limited efforts to create radio with appeal to the older market.

Radio stations appear to be targeted to the young, educated, upscale individuals who are rising through the ranks and spending in a significant way as they do.

Television Advertising

Clearly older Americans watch more television than younger people. National statistics on the viewing habits of the older consumer show they spend 70 percent more hours each day than the 18-to-34-year-old, according to Simmons Market Research. As the aging of America continues, television may have greater impact than it does now.

Television, especially the networks, has been reluctant to make changes which reflect these changing demographics. However, as the nation ages, so does the television viewing audience. But the television networks continue to promote their unique advantage based on the traditional demographics.

Mature market consultants Helen Harris and Vicki Thomas are convinced it would be in the best interests of the networks to incorporate data from Nielsen on the older demographics to make advertisers and ad agencies aware of the economic clout of this segment when it relates to product consumption and the attentiveness of the viewing audience.[13]

In their opinion, what types of shows do older viewers favor? According to TV Dimensions, these individuals are heavy daytime viewers and dominate the morning talk show audience, of which 59 percent of the male and 53 percent of the female viewers are 50-plus. This age group also constitutes the majority of game show audiences, weekly evening newscasts and prime time news magazine shows. And they make up the majority of the audience for soap operas, early evening police/adventure shows, prime time adventure shows and early evening sitcoms.

This audience not only has the time but is willing to make the time to view an advertising message selectively—a carry-over from the readership habits of print media. Not only does it spend more time, it is more attentive. This age group pays more attention to commercial messages since it is the least likely to get up and do something during a commercial, talk to others or switch channels.

They appear to be more benefit conscious than younger age segments, reviewing product and service messages to determine the unique benefits that can be provided to enrich their expanding lifestyle.

Telemarketing

The telephone is a primary medium in dealing with older bank customers. Because of the physical and sometimes psychological limitations of the senior market, a number of techniques need to be practiced

83

so that the telephone may be used effectively to service and sell the bank customer.

Telemarketing consultant Dr. Doreen V. Blanc, president, Aurora Marketing Management, Inc., Princeton, New Jersey, offers these tips to bankers dealing with older customers on the telephone on outbound calls:

- Because many have hearing problems, it is important to enunciate, speak loudly but not offensively. Early on, ask if the other person can hear you. Sometimes special phone equipment is used to help those hard of hearing. The recipient may need a second or two to adjust the equipment or hearing aid or to turn down distracting background noise such as radio or television. Verify that they can hear you but try to do it discreetly.

- At the beginning tell the person on the other end who you are and why you are calling. Older people can be impatient and want to know right away whom they are speaking with.

- Articulation is important; and so is being as logical as possible during the conversation. Sometimes older persons have problems dealing with abstract subjects in processing information.

- Plan the calls. Make just a few points. Remember that attention spans are limited. Follow up anything you have agreed to with a letter confirming it. Deal with more typical banking products on the phone; use direct mail to communicate more complex topics such as mutual funds.

- Speak into the telephone mouthpiece more directly than you ordinarily would. Don't cradle the telephone on a shoulder because it may cause a sound distortion.

- Tell the person why you are calling. Use common terms, not banker jargon. For example, use words like "savings accounts" not "time deposits."

- Come to the point quickly—without appearing to rush it. Ask for feedback with questions such as, "Tell me, Mrs. Smith, does this seem to be a banking service you could use?"

Her advice on in-bound telephone calls: Usually the recipient has only a second or two to realize that it is an older person. Again, make sure the caller can hear you. You can repeat what they have said to you, as a verification technique. Note that they may be confused or may be having difficulty hearing. Be sensitive to the person's needs even though they may simply want to vent frustrations they are experiencing. Be cautious about saying anything that would be taken by them as an insult.

Newsletters

Most marketers agree that newsletters are the basic communication tool with mature bank customers. They do much to develop and enhance customer loyalties. They provide exceptional cross-sell opportunities. They fit in well with the older customer's reading habits.

While newsletters are the primary means of communicating with the senior market, the banking industry is under severe pressures to make sure that any marketing expenditure is an economic one. John R. Klug, president, Continental Communications Group, Inc., Denver, sees more and more banks applying return-on-investment criteria when deciding on newsletters.

The industry is shifting from a communications to a selling mode in the use of newsletters. The purpose today is to develop newsletters that sell or get a response. "This is an inherent contradiction with the seniors market, " says Klug. "They do not want to be sold. They are skeptical of sales pitches. In effect, they have heard them all. The copy needs to be presented to them in way that makes sense to them and gives them assurances."

He recommends that banks design their newsletters differently for this market. Use larger type—a couple of point sizes larger but not so large as to be insulting. Overall design: Models, photography, illustrations and graphics have to be consistent. Use a more classical, but not staid, approach to graphics. The older customer will respond very well if the look is appropriate to the market.

Copy written by a 50-year-old often will be more on target than a younger person's. Consider using an older writer. His advice: Go out and talk to the market and see first-hand what they want. Do not use inappropriate language. Look at the seniors magazines as models.

Because seniors are avid readers and interested in a variety of subjects, topics may include opportunities for making more money, health care and preventative medicine, nutrition, exercise, travel tips, lifestyles, personalities, community service, hobbies, gardening, tax implications, updates on legislation at the state and national level affecting them, their social security, medical payments and life satisfaction subjects. The tone and look of the publication should reflect the bank—without using banker jargon.

If you are investigating the services of a senior newsletter publisher, Gary Ford, president, American Custom Publishing, offers this advice:[14]

- Don't be too self-serving. Present a proper mix of information of benefits to the senior particularly with information and marketing about the institution. Coupons, response cards and keyed telephone numbers are effective measuring tools.

- Before committing to a publisher, obtain and interview a list of their clients. Inquire about direct response methods and ways to measure the newsletter's effectiveness.

- Find out if you will have exclusive market rights to the copy. Determine how much customized work you want and what the extra costs are in customizing.

Tips on Advertising to Older Consumers

- Avoid exaggeration in communications. Mature market communications will come under close scrutiny. Avoid overstatements and generalities. The older consumer frequently goes back to the promotional message to see if the value promised in the marketing communications was delivered.

- Flashbacks, slice-of-life and nostalgic advertising can be effective. Avoid talking down to seniors. The printed word is significantly more credible to the mature customer, a group often described as "pure readers."

- Advertising should show how this will help them fulfill their dreams. The satisfied mature customer is one of the most important sources of word-of-mouth referrals. When they are appreciative of the product and service they tell others about it. Their influence on the younger market is sizable.

- The secret to any successful communication process is to understand how the recipient feels, thinks and acts. Customers and prospects in the mature market are no exception—as long as the marketer understands the significant differences between this market and others.

Our Recommendations

- ☐ Develop a sensitivity to the older customer segment by studying and analyzing the buying habits of mature adults. Subscribe to seniors publications to help develop awareness. (A list is included in the Appendix.) Hold in-bank staff awareness programs.

- ☐ Insist that the bank's advertising staff and ad agency understand that the market represents a unique challenge to them. Suggest that they attend seminars on marketing to seniors, subscribe to seniors publications and use their networks to build a data bank of relevant information.

- ☐ Review existing bank advertising to determine whether it is sending out negative messages to other market segments.

- ☐ Observe your bank personnel to determine their interactions with older customers and how they communicate with seniors.

- ☐ Review the physical look of all print advertising, promotional and communications material for seniors; check the design, type size, layout, illustrations, models, paper selection, legibility and clarity of message. Establish a seniors advisory panel to pre-test and post-test bank advertising.

☐ Conduct a review of the capabilities of the marketing and advertising staff regarding their ability to understand this market segment.

Notes

1. Summary of highlights from the American Society on Aging 13 Conference, "America, Business and Aging," *Selling to Seniors,* October, 1988.
2. James R. Lumpkin and Troy Festervand, "Purchase Information Sources of the Elderly," *Journal of Advertising Research,* December, 1987-January, 1988, P. 34.
3. Catherine A. Cole and Michael J. Houston, "Encoding and Media Effects on Consumer Learning Deficiencies in the Elderly," *Journal of Marketing Research,* February, 1987, P. 55.
4. Alan J. Greco, "Linking Dimensions of the Elderly Market to Market Planning," *Journal of Consumer Marketing,* Spring, 1987, P. 47.
5. James O. Gollub, "Business Opportunities among the Aging Population," SRI International Business Intelligence Program, Summer, 1984.
6. Anthony C. Ursic, Michael L. Ursic, Virginia L. Ursic, "A Longitudinal Study of the Use of the Elderly in Magazine Advertising," *Journal of Consumer Research,* June, 1986, P. 131.
7. Jeffry Scott, "The 55-Plus Crowd Is Still Kicking—and Buying," *Adweek,* October 31, 1988, P. 8.
8. Summary of highlights from the American Society on Aging Conference, "America, Business and Aging," *Selling to Seniors,* October, 1988.
9. R. J. Balkite, "Improving Ads to the 50 and Over Consumer," *Inside Print,* October, 1987, P. 87.
10. "The Who and How-to of the Nifty 50 + Market" Grey Advertising, NYC.
11. Helen Harris and Vicki Thomas, "Tune into the Mature Market," An unpublished manuscript, P. 6.
12. "Radio listens closely to the mature market," Eileen Norris, *Advertising Age,* October 19, 1987.
13. Harris and Thomas, Op. Cit., P. 7.
14. "Special Report—A Survey of Senior Newsletter Publications," *Mature Market Report,* April, 1988, P. 4.

8 Tracking Program Results

Common Mistakes

1   Not providing a system for monitoring and tracking results of the mature market program.

2   Failing to track information that tells what motivated the customer to sign up, deposit money or close an account.

3   Not tracking how the customer heard about the program to determine advertising effectiveness.

4   Lumping all new account information into one age category and not distinguishing the pre-retiree from the retiree.

5   Failure to provide top management with a monthly account of results by customer profile, account type, product and branch performance.

Our telephone surveys of banks offering various mature customer membership programs revealed that the sophistication of a computerized monthly tracking system does not exist.

Even FISI Madison Financial does not provide its users with a sophisticated software system to monitor and track club membership performance.

Monitoring and Tracking

Barnett Bank, Society Bank, Bank of Boston, and Premier Bank in Baton Rouge are a few of the banks that provide regular tracking reports on the club membership program's performance.

This information becomes invaluable to the marketing function because it serves as a guideline for change as well as providing regular reports which can be issued to top management.

Peggy Mastel, marketing officer at First National Bank in Grand Forks, North Dakota, described this situation: The 55 and Better program was launched in November, 1987, and in mid-1988 the bank had a number of changes. Top management was looking over all programs to determine where budgets could be reduced.

"We had all the information necessary to prove how well the program was performing, but it was not assembled in one place," said Mastel. "We were able to put together a comprehensive report that showed top management how valuable Club 55 and Better was." This kind of information may be necessary to save your program.

The Reporting System

The reporting system should be consistent at each branch, and should include the following:

- Membership listing: The membership listing provides an alphabetical listing of all customers in the program. Members should be assigned a membership number, and the date they signed up should be recorded. This listing is very helpful in building a mailing list. Most systems can convert this to mailing labels at any time.

- Customer profile: The customer profile provides demographic information. It should also provide information on what motivated the customer to open an account, how the customer learned about the program, what the sources of customer funds are, who opened the account (male, female, both), and age by demographic breakout as described in a previous chapter.

- Sales report: The most important source of information is a sales report. This tracks all the opening account information on all customers in the program. Each branch should have a separate code number to track similar information. The report should summarize the program by branch and provide month-to-month membership levels.

The marketer who wishes to call attention to the value and results of the seniors program is strongly advised to create a tracking system. Most CEOs determine budget allocations based on the performance of programs. A monthly computer print-out demonstrating performance would serve to resolve any doubt about the value the mature customer has to the bank's bottom line.

The Tracking Form

While it can be time consuming, tracking forms should be filled out by each customer service representative signing up a senior account. A model form is shown in Figure 1.

According to Duane Kimball, CEO of Emanacom, a Hampton, New Hampshire based tracking software firm that monitors the Richer Life program for Bank 5, "A bank offering a senior club membership program needs to look at three things to implement a tracking system; 1) a need to plan what information goes to whom, 2) a means to anticipate information needs of the program and 3) what special customized features the bank is looking for on the mature customers' accounts." Emanacom's system is able to track sales in 10 different demographic categories.

Frank Moro, vice president of Barry Leeds & Associates, a New York City based sales tracking firm says, "There is no one right way to track sales activity, but rather there are many right ways depending on the specific objective of the senior club membership program."

Figure 1

Client Interview

Customer Name		Type of Customer □ New □ Existing	Date
Primary Reason	Service Sold	$ Amount (No Cents)	1. Source of Internal Funds Transfer
1 □ Checking	10 □ DDA Acct 11 □ NOW Acct 12 □ Special Checking 13 □ Money Market		1 □ Checking 2 □ Savings 3 □ Money Market 4 □ CD
2 □ Savings	20 □ Super Saver 21 □ Statement Savings		2. Source of External Funds Transfer
3 □ CD/IRA	30 □ CD 31 □ Jumbo CD (100,000 +) 32 □ IRA—All Types 33 □ CD Rollover		1 □ Savings Bank 2 □ Commercial Bank 3 □ Brokerage Firm 4 □ Credit Union
4 □ Credit	40 □ Privilege Checking 41 □ MasterCard 42 □ Visa 43 □ Personal Loan 44 □ Boat Loan 45 □ Auto Loan 46 □ Credit on Demand 47 □ Student Loan		3. Customer Type 1 □ Mature Market 2 □ Empty Den 3 □ Married w/ children 4 □ Newlyweds 5 □ Young Single 6 □ Commercial
5 □ Shelter	50 □ Mortgage 51 □ Home Equity		
6 □ Business	60 □ Business Checking 61 □ Business Money Market 62 □ Business Savings 63 □ Commercal Loan 64 □ Business Revolving Credit 65 □ Keogh 66 □ SEP 67 □ Letter of Credit 68 □ Payroll Services		
7 □ Relationship Products	70 □ Select Accounts 71 □ ATM Card 72 □ Student Plus 73 □ Special Banking		
8 □ Other Products	80 □ Safe Deposit Box 81 □ Christmas Club		

Total New Services Sold	Branch	Employee No. ——————— Manager's Initials	Employee Name
	Branch Name		

Barry Leeds Associates, unlike Emanacom, is a service bureau. Many banks subscribe to the firm to receive monthly tracking reports on their senior program's performance. According to Frank Moro, very few banks do lifestyle tracking. Moro believes that much more should be done because tracking enables a bank to make changes and improvements where needed.

Measurement is the foundational step. Once the foundation has been established, the critical steps of recognition, reward and goal setting for the club membership program can be implemented. How quickly or slowly these next steps are phased in is a function of how well the bank adapts to the first phase of measurement. The key is to realize that all of these are vital components of a sales tracking and monitoring system, and without each piece, it will be difficult to effectively weave sales into the fabric of the bank.

Tracking Problems

The most frequent problem encountered in implementing tracking programs in banks is that the staff doesn't truly understand the concepts and vocabulary, from tellers on up through senior management. The concept of tracking is very new to the banking industry. Moro says, "Banks have not been conditioned to develop programs based on a sales culture."

In 1969, Barry Leeds gave a speech at a national industry conference in which he said "the missing link in sales development in the banking industry is a quantifiable, reliable sales measurement system." Twenty years later, there are an estimated 2,000 financial institutions actually tracking sales and cross-selling on an individual salesperson basis. There are more than 25,000 banks and savings and loans in business and less than 1,500 of them are actually measuring sales performance on an ongoing basis.

According to Frank Moro, some of the more important reasons given for the lack of developing or providing a sales program are: lack of management commitment, poor staff attitude, inadequate training and lack of a means to measure sales. A proper sales measurement technique or system will soon become a priority as banks strive to achieve greater profitability in financial product areas.

Guidelines for Developing a Tracking Program

The following questions and issues are considered when Barry Leeds & Associates develops a tracking program.

Program Overview

- What department, branch, or type of account will be measured?
- Will all of the employee groups participating in the cross-sales and/or referral program be included initially or will some be phased in at a later time?

- What employee positions will be included in the program?
- What products and services will be included in the program?
- Will input documents, for various employee groups to be measured, need to be developed?

Customer Interview Form

- Will you use a log format or a single sheet for each customer interviewed?
- How many duplicate copies will the customer interview form have?
- How many duplicate copies will the referral form have?
- What information will be listed on the referral form?

Paper Flow

- What is the paper flow—the distribution and routing—for the new accounts form?
- What is the paper flow—the distribution and routing—for the referral form?
- Will input documents be collected from sales and/or referral employees daily or weekly?
- What are the check points to ensure that documents are completed correctly?
  – Manager
  – Support staff
- What is the cut-off time by which all input documents must be received so sales are included in month-end figures?
- What happens if documents are received after this time?

Referrals

- What is the time limit for giving credit for a sale that results from a referral?
- If an employee makes a referral suggestion, but the client doesn't bring in the referral form, will the employee be credited for the sale?

Program Administration

- Who will be responsible for overall management of the measurement program?
- What will this person's responsibilities include?

Reports

- How often will reports be distributed?
- Who will receive reports?
- Which reports will be distributed to whom?

Problem Resolution

■ How much time does the employee have to take action to ensure that an error is corrected?

■ What documentation must be presented, and to whom is this information presented, to correct an error?

■ How will this correction be reflected in the measurement figures?

Auditing Procedures

■ What is the schedule for auditing the measurement program?
 – Which documents will be reviewed?
 – How often will these documents be checked?
 – How many documents will be checked, and how often will they be selected?

■ Who will be responsible for these audits?

■ What other check points can be developed to ensure the integrity of the data?

■ What is the bank's policy if managers and or/employees are discovered misreporting their sales activity?

■ How will this policy be communicated to the staff?

Moro advises banks to realize that they won't know all the answers. Realize also that there isn't just one answer, but a multitude of possible choices depending on the bank's marketing objectives. Sometimes it will require experimenting to determine the best approach. Other times, a method will work initially, but as your sales management strategies become more sophisticated, there will be a need to refine the sales tracking methods. The sales tracking system should be flexible and responsive so it can meet the needs of the ever changing marketplace.

Our Recommendations

☐ A sophisticated means of monitoring the performance of the mature market program must be a priority.

☐ Contact tracking organizations to schedule a presentation on the forms, benefits, results and needs of a good tracking system.

☐ Talk to other banks that have tracking systems in place to determine what your bank's needs are.

☐ Be sure to include information on the tracking report that provides information on what accounts were closed and why money was withdrawn.

☐ To evaluate advertising effectiveness, include information on the form as to how the mature market member heard about the program benefits.

93

9 Staffing

Common Mistakes

1. Underestimating the amount of staff time it takes to effectively coordinate a mature market membership program.

2. Expecting the senior program product area to succeed with the marketing department coordinating the activities while having to be responsible for other priorities within the bank as well.

3. Not receiving a commitment from top management to support the activities, product development, and coordination of a seniors program on a full-time basis.

4. Overlooking the retired employee or customer as a source for part-time or volunteer help.

5. Not incorporating the seniors program and services into the bank's overall corporate objectives.

6. Placing the senior program support in a department other than marketing or retail banking.

The previous chapters provided facts and statistics about the size and future growth of the mature customer segment. FISI Madison Financial estimates that there are currently 1,500 banks providing special programs for the valued mature customer base; our projections indicate that within five years the number will double, and within ten years virtually all banks will be providing special programs and services to attract, maintain and develop older customer deposits and loyal relationships.

As it is now, the average bank customer over age 50 has at least three different accounts in three or more different institutions. The average balance of each account is $6,000. The customer over the age of 50 has an average savings account of $25,000.

As more and more banks begin to offer programs designed to attract senior customers, a commitment to staffing will be a must to ensure that proper administration, coordination and on-going development is maintained. The competition in the future within the financial field will intensify. As that happens the key to the program's success will be differentiation and adequate staffing. Bank management can no longer afford to have the responsibility for the senior program area belong to one marketing person, who also performs several other functions within the bank.

Many banks have had to downsize staff in recent years, which has greatly affected the marketing area. According to our telephone interviews, those remaining in marketing functions currently perform several

94

responsibilities within the bank, therefore giving only as little as 80 hours per year to coordinate the senior program's activities.

The coordinated efforts of a well-run seniors program become even more clouded with banks that have a decentralized marketing function. Many banks that have several hundred branches or cross state lines have even more difficulty maintaining program continuity because of the distances and other priorities within the region or branch.

Several banks using turn-key programs such as FISI Madison Financial, the Richer Life program, or other providers have expected the seniors package of services to run effectively and efficiently without providing or designating a full-time coordinator to work as the bank's liaison with the customers, the turn-key provider and top management within the bank structure. The turn-key provider often becomes a "quick fix" to the problem of serving customers 50 and older while requiring a minimum of staff time.

Establishing a Full-Time Senior Coordinator Position

According to our telephone interviews, only two percent of banks currently have a full-time staff person who is solely responsible for the administration, development and coordination of the senior program area.

The greatest concentration of full-time directors or program coordinators for the senior market area can be found in Florida, where there is a greater concentration of people over 50. Banks and financial institutions in general have become very competitive in their efforts to attract, build and maintain older customer deposits.

Society Bank in Cleveland, Ohio recently created a new position to be responsible for the development, coordination and administration of the bank's Prime Advantage Program. The position of Senior Vice President/Market Manager—Prime Advantage reports to the executive vice president of the bank.

First Bank System in Minneapolis has a Vice President of Segment Management and Planning. One of the positions that reports to the vice president is a Segment Manager who is responsible for the program development of the senior product area.

Premier Bank in Baton Rouge, Louisiana has a Marketing Director who develops the umbrella mature market program for Premier Partners coordinators to administer at the various branches. The Marketing Director reports to the vice president of marketing.

A number of FISI Madison Financial bank users have established 55 and Better coordinators. Examples include First National Bank in Grand Forks, North Dakota and FirsTier Bank in Omaha, Nebraska.

The Richer Life program, a mature market turn-key service, has a prerequisite that all those wanting to subscribe to the franchise designate a full-time coordinator to manage the program.

John Migliaccio, director of special projects for the New York City based Retirement Advisors, stated in a phone interview that his firm experienced several situations where the vice president at the bank was interested in developing a seniors program that would include pre-retirement seminars for those customers. "The vice president receives an offer to go to another bank and the program plans come to a halt because the bank's program is personality driven. Top management has made a major mistake by not incorporating the program as part of the overall strategy, to ensure ongoing service even when a key person leaves the bank," says Migliaccio.

As more and more banks recognize the value of the mature market customer base and as the marketing emphasis shifts from youth to older consumers, proper staffing will be vital to the program's success. Our estimates are that within five years most banks will have at least one full-time position that will be responsible for the senior customer base.

"55 and Better" Coordinator's Role and Responsibilities

FISI Madison Financial provides a menu of services that a bank can elect to purchase in order to implement a seniors program for customers 55 and over. FISI currently serves 500 banks and has over 1,000,000 members in those programs.

According to Marcy Massie, executive director of FISI Madison Financial, "the majority of banks begin the program by instituting the $100 minimum balance checking account, which entitles customers 55 and over to a variety of membership benefits and privileges."

As the bank selects various products from the FISI menu of services, the role and responsibility of a designated bank coordinator becomes even more critical to the program's overall success. Massie indicated that most banks experience tremendous growth in the first year with the program. It gets harder as the program matures to continue to build and increase customer relationships. A good coordinator is one who will work hard to develop programs to keep the customer list growing.

A bank's coordinator with FISI Madison Financial has the following duties and responsibilities:

- Serves as advisor and counselor to customers 55 and over.

- Qualifies all new customers who have opened an account with personal phone calls, visits or mailings.

- Plans and implements meaningful programs such as seminars on financial planning, health care, budgeting, how to live alone, or osteoporosis.

- Plans and implements social activities (which FISI recommends only after obtaining 8,000-10,000 members) that include one-day bus tours, luncheons with speakers, "senior" proms, luncheon with the bank president, 10-cent "classic" movies, etc.

- Develops and implements a plan for increasing membership to the program as an ongoing part of the program.

- Plans to spend at least two or three days at selected branches answering questions and helping customers better understand the program benefits.
- Develops and plans the program announcements for placement in local newspapers about the program's activities and benefits.
- Sets up a tracking system to monitor and report program results.

Massie believes that the coordinator should also become an internal program advocate promoting the benefits and results to top management with monthly memos and financial data to ensure bank-wide recognition for the program's contribution to the overall bottom line.

The Position Within the Bank

The first objective in establishing the position of a senior services program coordinator is to determine where the function belongs and fits in the bank. There is no right formula, and each bank must staff the position according to the personnel guidelines established by the bank.

Ideally the position or positions should have a direct line of communications to top management. The position will work closely with a number of divisions in the bank, including marketing, research, public relations, top management, personnel, trusts, training, and new business development.

The ideal is seldom achieved, especially since new staff positions may have been frozen by banks that have recently downsized. Another good place for the position is within a centralized marketing department, with the function reporting directly to the vice president or director. The position should be given officer status and should be a staff position, not a line position. Obviously, the position should be appropriate to the organization's structure.

If the marketing department is decentralized, the position should then be placed in the Retail Customer Banking Division.

Job Description and Qualifications

The duties and responsibilities for the senior services coordinator will vary depending on what the bank has already accomplished in the development of a mature market program. In most instances the program will already have achieved some momentum and growth as a result of having the position function within the marketing department.

The title of the position should be directly linked to the name selected for the bank's Senior Program, such as the "Value Partners" Coordinator, Director, or Assistant Vice President.

Since the staff position will be interacting with the customers 50 and over, care should be given to avoid such titles as senior service coordinator. Many customers in this age group do not appreciate being designated "seniors" and would not be receptive to discussing their membership needs with the "senior" coordinator.

The individual selected for the position should possess excellent communications skills. It will be very important that the bank select a candidate who will create a favorable impression not only with the customer group, but also with the community. The candidate will be required to speak to various civic clubs, Senior Centers, and organizations about the program's benefits and uniqueness.

The individual will be key to creating a great deal of outside visibility to the press, TV talk shows, presentations at senior clubs, Rotary, Lions and the local Chamber of Commerce.

Another important ingredient in selecting the right person is to make sure others at the bank who will be working closely with this person feel comfortable with the candidate. This position will interact with almost all divisions at the bank.

If the bank has a mature market program or is about to launch one, a selection group should be established to review and interview selected candidates for the position. This should include a designated individual or individuals from the senior program so they feel involved in the selection process.

Recruiting Candidates for the Position

The candidate selected to be responsible for the bank's mature market customer program may already be on staff. This person may be someone who has been wearing several hats which have included the development, coordination and administration of the senior program. The benefit to the bank of hiring from within is obvious. There will be little training and orientation needed to understand the bank's structure, names and acronyms. The person already has a commitment and understanding to the mature market customer needs, but hasn't had the opportunity to be devoted to the program on a full-time basis.

If the bank elects to recruit someone from the outside, careful consideration should be given to the credentials and qualifications required to staff the position.

The position should require three areas of expertise:

1. Previous work experience with a financial institution. This could include work at a bank, savings & loan, credit union or investment firm.
2. Marketing expertise, as demonstrated by a college degree in marketing or experience in developing a successful seniors program at another financial institution. The individual could also have worked as a brand manager with a pharmaceutical or consumer products company responsible for products targeted to consumers 50 and over.
3. Knowledge about the field of gerontology. This requires an understanding of the psychology and physiology of aging. Experience could have been obtained working at a well-run senior center, continuing care facility or hospital or from study in the field of gerontology. Consider an individual who may have

worked for an organization that specializes in the older market segment such as AARP, Mature Outlook, the National Council on Aging, the State Department on Aging or its Area Agencies on Aging.

The bank should also review past employment records for officers and key personnel who have retired, and who might be interested in the newly created position at the bank. This, in fact, could be a great resource for the bank to tap, since they have a knowledge of the bank and experience in retirement-related issues.

This retired pool of individuals could also be a source of part-time assistance to the program in selected branch areas.

Sample Job Description

Position Title:
Director, Assistant Vice President or Vice President of (name of bank senior program)

Qualifications:
At least 5 years previous work experience in the marketing department at a bank, savings & loan, insurance company or investment firm.

At least two years experience coordinating a senior program or product at a financial institution or pharmaceutical or consumer products company targeted to individuals 50 and older.

A degree or certification in the field of gerontology not required, but helpful. A degree in marketing.

Duties and Responsibilities:
This position will be responsible for the program development, coordination, product development, communications, marketing, monitoring and tracking of (name of bank's senior program), which serves customers and potential customers 50 and older.

Responsibilities include:
1. Provide ongoing market research to determine customer satisfaction for the senior program, products and services provided, and future enhancements.
2. Maintain active and regular competitive analysis of similar programs offered by other banks, credit unions, savings and loans and other non-bank competitors.
3. Establish and develop responsive communications vehicles for existing and potential customers 50 and older.
4. Work with the advertising agency or in-house creative staff to develop, create and implement attractive advertisements designed to create greater awareness of the bank's unique senior programs, services and benefits.
5. Develop and implement special value-added program benefits such as seminars, lectures, workshops and schools on retirement related issues.
6. Evaluate and add special features to improve the overall program, to build and maintain loyal, lasting customer relationships.
7. Provide management with monthly updates on the program's results and product performance.

8. Represent the bank at civic, community and senior sponsored functions throughout the state.
9. Interact with and coordinate activities with all departments within the bank, including outside resource personnel necessary to the program's success such as research firms, advertising agencies, public relations firms, consultants and vendors that might provide program enhancements.
10. Provide and establish a system to coordinate the senior program activities of (name of senior program) at all bank branches throughout the system to ensure ongoing growth in membership.
11. Train and orient customer service representatives on the program products, benefits and services.
12. Develop customer service representatives sales incentives throughout the bank branch system to increase membership sign-up and cross-sell other bank products and services.
13. Establish (name of bank senior program) advisory board to meet regularly to evaluate program and membership benefits and to determine future program direction.
14. Stay current and aware of continuing changing demographics trends. Keep top management informed about the changes with recommended suggestions on what actions the bank should be taking to be more responsive in meeting those needs.

Position reports to:
Vice President/Director of Marketing

Salary range:
(As determined by the personnel policies of the bank)

Retired Bank Personnel

As the population ages, and customers continue to grow older as well, many banks are going to have to start utilizing the tremendous resources provided by older workers.

Any bank may have an untapped pool of experienced personnel who have retired from their positions. These individuals offer potential part-time workers on the senior program helping older bank customers deal with retirement related issues.

They could be perfect representatives to work at the branches on a regularly scheduled part-time basis—perhaps 1:00-3:00 p.m. on Tuesday and Thursdays. They would be trained to explain the benefits of the senior program of services to customers 50 and older. In addition, special training sessions could be provided for these workers so they could answer questions older bank customers may have regarding Social Security, Medicare, or resources available for seniors in the community.

Special commission incentives could be established for signing up a new member or for encouraging an increased deposit into one of the savings account programs available in the bank's senior program.

Other functions that branch senior service representatives could perform would include coordination and organization of local one-day field trips and tours, and special events that might include a day at the

100

movies to watch cinema classics. They might also begin to organize overnight trips and weekend trips to more distant locations.

The full-time staff position would provide regular training programs for the senior branch coordinators, as well as provide the incentives necessary to keep the retired individual involved and committed to the bank's senior services program.

One Organization's Experience

Western Savings and Loan Association in Phoenix, Arizona, hires older workers for full-time positions and retirees for part-time or on-call employment with benefits based on work hours and earnings.

When the company began to enter the retirement market, management became aware of the need for heavier staffing and started to hire workers in the same age group as their customers. The program has been successfully implemented ever since. According to the vice president of employee relations, older people often are interested in greater customer interaction. They spend more time with a customer and they relate better to the needs of retired people than many younger employees. They are representative of the communities they serve.

Part-time and on-call employees work during peak business hours, at lunch time and weekends. The majority are employed as tellers, the rest as hosts and hostesses at the "Westerners Club" organized for large-deposit customers.

The company provides fully paid health insurance for all full-time workers. Part-time employees may pay for insurance coverage. The company has a pension plan, as well as profit sharing. Employees past the age of 60 cannot participate in the pension plan, but are entitled to profit sharing. All employees receive sick leave, vacations and holiday pay, prorated in the case of part-time employment.

Other employee benefits include reduced mortgage rates, free checking, eight percent off the normal interest rate on credit cards, and a Social Security supplement for eligible retirees. The company estimates the benefits cost over 30 percent of the payroll dollar. The vice president describes the benefits as geared toward longevity. The company feels the obligation to provide for its employees and the employees consider the company as a career. Increased loyalty and reduced turnover are thought to compensate for benefit costs.

Sample Job Description

Position Title:
Branch (name of senior program) Service Representative

Qualifications:
Retired bank employee or other interested individual who has a thorough knowledge of Social Security, Medicare and community programs designed to help older bank customers better understand retirement related issues.

Must have good interpersonal and communication skills. Must be willing to travel on local trips and to attend functions within the community that are geared to the senior citizen.

Hours:
Four days a week—1:00 to 3:00 on Tuesdays and Thursdays, 10:00 to noon on Mondays and Wednesdays

Duties and Responsibilities:
1. Operate and manage the branch (name of senior program) desk.
2. Answer questions older customers may have about filing out a Medicare form or filing for Social Security.
3. Recruit and sign up new members to the (name of senior program).
4. Arrange and accompany members on one-day trips and tours to various places of interest.
5. Serve as host or hostess at special planned branch retirement seminars, workshops or lectures sponsored by the bank.
6. Conduct face-to-face surveys with bank members and non-members to determine their satisfaction or dissatisfaction with bank services and membership privileges.
7. Take deposits and transactions from members of the club during scheduled hours.
8. Represent branch at all bank-sponsored community senior programs.
9. Issue a monthly report to the director of (name of senior program) on results, membership sign-up, anticipated problems or special opportunities the branch should explore as a benefit to members.
10. Attend special training and orientation sessions at the bank headquarters on a quarterly basis.

Position reports to:
(Name of senior program) Director.

Salary and benefits according to hours worked.

The Senior Advisory Board

As more and more financial institutions target the mature market, program benefits and services will become very much alike. Soon the mature customer will become oversaturated with membership opportunities, special invitations, seminars, newsletters and information professing to help them take charge of their financial life, and they may become jaded to program offers. Mature market customers will begin to develop an "everyone wants my money" attitude and will become much more critical of offers for membership privileges. This feeling will grow even more intense with the baby boomer generation, rapidly approaching 50, which is used to being catered to.

Bank programs targeting the mature market customer will have to constantly evaluate the program results and monitor the behavior of older members in the program. The astute marketer will always want to be on the lookout for that special touch, the new opportunity and that something different to breathe life and excitement into the program. Differentiation will be the key. Uniqueness will be rewarded with customer satisfaction. One cannot expect to implement a program and feel that the mature market customer needs have been met permanently.

One of the best ways to stay current with members of the program is to create a special advisory board or council that would meet on a quarterly basis to review the program, evaluate the services and benefits, provide feedback for improvement and new enhancements, and also let the bank know what the competition is doing.

The council representatives should be selected based on criteria set by the bank. The representatives should include a good cross-section of the mature market, like a pre-retiree, a retired professional, a retired plant or skilled laborer, a widow, a teacher and a business owner. The advisory board should also include the program director, several branch representatives and a representative from the bank's top management. The council should have a chairman.

Highlights of meetings and findings from the group should be reported to the membership via the newsletter, magazine or special letter from the program coordinator.

The important point to remember here is involvement and participation. If the program is really a membership, then members should have a say in the types of programs and services that are offered.

The incentive for council or advisory board participation is a dinner, special discounts, and the prestige of being on the selected board.

The advisory board should have a fair amount of turnover in order to get fresh ideas. Therefore, the position should be for one year. At the end of that year, a new council or advisory board should be recruited.

Budgeting

Each bank will have to determine the yearly budget to promote, manage and maintain a successful ongoing mature market program.

There is no established formula with banks that have already implemented seniors programs. In our telephone interviews with selected banks, we found that the formula used varied from one percent to 20 percent of the overall marketing budget. Our surveys also revealed that most banks providing seniors programs do not have the total budget dollars figured for all departments involved, which include staff time, administration and handling. And, in fact, most banks were only able to give the figure as it related to the promotional expenditure.

We also found out from our telephone interviews that many banks provide an initial big promotional push which usually lasts one year. Other priorities develop at the bank and the mature market program budget gets reduced at a critical time when on-going dollars are needed to support the continued growth and success of the program. The best results are achieved during the first year. It is very important to allocate enough budgetary dollars to maintain the momentum and to develop new strategies to continue to increase membership deposits and services.

The budgetary line items that should be included are:

- Salaries and related expenses
- Travel expenses to the various branch offices
- General office supplies
- Printing and design of all materials
- Speciality/premiums
- Administrative expenses—newsletter, telephone, postage, dues, subscriptions and books
- Public relations expenses
- Advertising and promotion expenses
- Training for customer contact people
- Consultant fees, agency expenses
- Local service fees

Our Recommendations

☐ Give the senior market segment the priority it deserves in the bank. Incorporate the objectives of the program into the bank's overall corporate goals.

☐ Provide the necessary staffing required to build the seniors program, recruit members, increase deposits and cross-sell other bank services.

☐ Provide for and include a system for tracking and monitoring the results of the program. Top management understands and responds to numerical data.

☐ Establish a working team within the bank to be responsible for the mature market customer base, consisting of representatives from marketing, retail banking, top management, research, trust, human resources, and new product development.

☐ Don't tie the mature market program just to a special membership. Be sure to reach out into the community by sponsoring special events and programs which the mature market frequents.

☐ Build a file and talent bank consisting of retirees from the bank and retired bank customers to work as customer service representatives.

☐ Hire retirees on a part-time basis to operate a designated desk for members of mature market program.

☐ Stay current by subscribing to special newsletters and magazines specializing in the mature market segment.

- [ ] Develop a new network of contacts in the mature market segment by joining organizations that specialize in this market segment.

- [ ] Subscribe to special research reports on the mature market segment.

- [ ] Constantly monitor the bank's senior program to improve, add value and differentiate from others offering a similar package.

- [ ] Establish an advisory board or council to meet regularly to provide input for improvement, monitor results and build more value added services to the package.

- [ ] Network with other banks and financial institutions that have senior programs. Find out what works, what doesn't, and where the senior market is headed.

- [ ] Be creative and imaginative with the senior program. Just because the bank down the street has implemented a program doesn't mean you have to mirror the concept. Originality and uniqueness will be rewarded.

- [ ] Audit the senior program area on a yearly basis to determine new directions and provide additional programs.

10 Developing Employee Sensitivity to Mature Customers

Common Mistakes

1 Failure to understand that bank employees are a more critical link to the older customer than they are to other customer segments, and to take actions to ensure their support.

2 Lack of communication with bank employees systemwide about the bank's strategic direction relative to the seniors market.

3 Failure to understand that employees need training in understanding the physical and psychological differences in dealing with older customers.

4 Lack of appreciation that a number of key customer contact personnel have difficulty dealing with the mature person.

5 No formal training programs for employees to develop sensitivity toward the older customer.

6 Failure to develop a customer-friendly physical atmosphere through branch design and environment.

We are all discovering that retail banking relies heavily on the ability of the bank's marketing arm—the employees—to make a difference. The promise inherent in all the bank's marketing efforts is hollow if the delivery through exceptional service is not provided by the customer service personnel. Interest in developing bank-wide service and selling standards throughout the industry is the major issue for retail bankers across the country.

Developing greater understanding and appreciation of the older bank customer fits well with the bank's efforts to improve the quality of its service, but there is limited internal action being taken to create awareness of the differences in dealing with older customers and encourage cross-selling of bank products. If employees are part of a bank that is aware of and conducting training programs, it is because the bank is located in a Sunbelt location with heavy emphasis on the pre-retired and retired market. Or the bank is one of those few which recognize the enormous future potential in dealing with older consumers.

There is no question that the success of the bank's mature market program rests primarily with the customer contact personnel. It is interesting to note that mature customers maintain banking relationships at a number of financial institutions. Customer contact personnel who are trained and motivated can be the most effective way to convince older customers to consolidate or increase their accounts with the bank.

The Right People, The Right Approach

Building or enhancing the bank's efforts with its mature customer base is contingent upon the bank employees' ability to deal with customers in their 50s through 80s. Just as all bank employees are not well suited for dealing with customers in a service capacity or in a sales role, all bank employees are not well suited to deal with older customers. Still they are critically important.

As well-regarded bank consultant George Rieder puts it:[1]

In the financial services business, the individual delivering the service becomes a differentiating individual and an integral part of the service. It is the sum total of individual service contacts between employees and customers that gives the bank its character, its reputation and its distinctiveness.... Employees refer to "my customer" and, in turn, customers refer to "my bank."

Further, he points out that in commercial banking there exists a personal relationship duplicated by few other businesses or professions. Such factors as friendliness, courtesy, attention to problem solving, efficiency and knowledgeable personnel represent value, not cliches, in the banking industry. These values are essential as banks compete for customers in an increasingly deregulated industry.

Dealing with intense and disruptive organizational change and restructuring is a major event in the banking industry.[2] A marketing officer in a mid-sized, Midwest bank states that his bank wants employees to understand that the bank needs them to think about their role differently. Banking, as he sees it, has changed and the bank is no longer the protected, patriarchal organization that many of those bank employees grew up with. All that has changed, he says. "We need them to understand they have to contribute to the improvement of customer services."

Employee Age, Customer Age

At many banks nearly 70 percent of the bank's employees are under 30 years of age.[3] While the average age may be higher for customer service representatives, the point is that many younger people often do not understand the needs of the mature customer nor do they have the time or patience to do a better job of dealing with them.

Frequently, younger people are not knowledgeable about the attitudes, interests, needs and wants of people over the age of 50. While some employees are especially adept at dealing with an older customer, others come across as flippant and impatient with individuals who do not move at a faster pace. It is up to the bank to design training programs directed toward employees so they can understand how to deal with older customers. Then, it is up to supervisory management to make sure it is being done.

"Consumers like to buy from people like themselves," says Jim Schneider.[4] Personality fit is more important to sales achievement than age, gender or sales experience.

Most banks try to sell seniors with the wrong sales staff. Young, competitive people who think of themselves as high commission, "fast close," super sellers are not likely to fare well in the senior lane, where patience, service and relationship are of primary importance. Rather, the peak performers are those who are assertive, with strong empathy, seeing themselves as problem solvers rather than sellers. Increasingly, banks are turning to mature sellers, even part-timers, to sell to seniors.

One approach for a bank that is making a long-term commitment to this market is to look at the bank's hiring practices and policies to attract competent staff who will aid the development of mature customer programs. Those banks that have performed well in dealing with a more mature customer base are those which have made special efforts to help customer service representatives understand and know how to deal with older customers.

The Four Faces of the New Senior

There are sharp differences in attitudes in dealing with the mature customer compared with other, younger customers. Chapter 1 is devoted to an understanding of the older bank customer and should be used as reference and for developing employee training programs. One model that may be helpful to bank employees in developing a better understanding of the seniors market and becoming more aware and sensitive to their needs is provided by David Wolfe.[5]

1. Creativity and intellectual involvement. The New Senior is a member of the most information-driven segment of our society (when information is not related to their livelihood.) Their favorite TV shows are news programs and documentaries....They read magazines and newspapers (more than younger segments). They travel to expand their intellectual horizons versus young people who travel to escape. They are signing up at colleges and universities by the tens of thousands. They are creative about shaping their lives and are intellectually involved in life. They employ this bent in their consumer behavior patterns, especially in their more detailed readership of promotional materials—provided it is lean on hyperbole.

2. Experience and wisdom and the desire to share. The now famous TV commercials from McDonald's showing the retired gentleman going back to work symbolizes this face for the "common folk" in a way that has caught the fancy of the country reportedly not only produced senior employees (the original purpose of the commercial) but increased restaurant patronage by seniors who

apparently liked the way the commercial pictured seniors. We often talk about the experience and wisdom of older people but generally ignore their desire to share it.

3. Vitality and productivity. We see a 75-year-old who is "active" and say, "That is remarkable." Well, more and more older people are being described as being remarkable. One 84-year-old woman said she was tired of being referred to as remarkable. "Hell, I am just an 84-year-old version of my 20-year-old self—I was always remarkable," she explains. Most seniors want to continue producing something of value—it's the only route to self-esteem. Self-esteem does not derive from one's consumption patterns.

The over-emphasis on leisure in marketing living environments is contrary to this image of productivity. A 1977 survey by the Roper Organization found 95 percent of seniors did not want to move to a seniors community. A 1986 study by SRI found over 80 percent of seniors felt there was too much emphasis on recreation in marketing communications for senior communities.

4. Compassion for others and concern for the world about them. Seniors are our best citizens. They vote at a higher rate than any other age group and they are more heavily involved in "good works" than the rest of the population. While one may argue, "That's because they have more time," it may be because they care more. Otherwise, they would do as most non-seniors erroneously think they do—play full-time and love it.

The bank employee who understands these attributes of the older customer holds an edge in the relationship with seniors. When talking with older customers, the bank employee can listen patiently to the wisdom older persons are imparting. The employee can make references to the vitality of the senior in conversations with them.

And the employee can be empathetic with the mature customer when the person describes their feelings about the world in which they live. In any kind of customer relationship, what is of interest to the customer is important; not what is important to the bank teller or the customer service representative. Understanding attitudes and values is important because it explains why people do things. A veteran senior marketer, Kurt Medina, senior vice president, National Liberty Marketing, Valley Forge, Pennsylvania, has this advice for bank employees:[6] "Seniors do not value surprises, so promise and deliver what is expected. Quality is number one with them, so they are willing to pay more to get more. Older customers view debt as sin, so they do not purposefully get into it. Older females are more likely to accept change, especially if they can get their spouses to change. Older people will not try something new without much thought and examination, so do not try to close quickly on them. Seniors like to communicate one on one, so deal with them on a personal basis. The older person's home is where their roots are, so they do not want to leave. For seniors, a referral from a friend means more than the effect of 20-30 ads, so they have more comfort with local organizations."

Developing Employee Awareness

Understanding the mature customer means understanding the physical differences between older and younger customers. There are many graphic examples of training sessions in which employees develop empathy for older customers. For example, to develop employee understanding of these differences, Great Western Savings Bank in Bellevue, Washington, conducted a series of seminars titled "Sensitivity to Aging," for more than a hundred employees. The approach they used was startlingly different.[7]

Employees pulled on rubber gloves, stuffed their ears with cotton balls and dimmed the lights. They were given directions to read in which the type was so small it was almost unreadable. Then they attempted to fill out deposit slips.

It worked. According to one attendee, "The rubber gloves let us know how difficult it was to write with arthritis and the cotton served to deaden the sound. I couldn't hear, see or feel a darned thing and I found out how difficult it was to fill out paperwork."

The sessions were run one hour a day for three days by a social worker who specializes in the problems of seniors. The seminars showed employees how to minimize frustration among the elderly who often have difficulties carrying out banking transactions. Tellers, customer service representatives and branch managers participated.

The employees found the training impressed them. "Seniors have certain limitations and we have to deal with those limitations because they are our customers," said an employee participating in the training. They found it normal for the bank employee to feel stress when dealing with the elderly. The program focuses on handling the stress and not letting it affect their response.

More than 50 percent of Great Western's customers are more than 55 years old. The seminar was suggested to the thrift by the Senior Service Center in Seattle which realized the banking community had no formal structure to help the elderly handle banking transactions.

Scudder, Stevens & Clark, Long Beach, California, which provides investment services to AARP members, holds an introduction to gerontology session as part of its month-long training program for telephone representatives. The program is meant to increase empathy and deepen the understanding of telemarketers. Gerontologists often put petroleum jelly on the glasses or tape the fingers of those attending the classes to simulate what the elderly have to deal with.

Training the Contact Personnel

When a bank determines it will devote resources to a segment of the customer base, it must communicate the objective to all employees—

especially those who are on the firing line such as customer sales and customer service representatives.

Banks approach the task from different points of view. One of those who has been a leader in marketing to seniors is H. George Kalluskey, vice president, public relations, Santa Barbara Bank & Trust, Santa Barbara, California, a bank with $600 million in assets and nine offices.

"Our Gang—The Over 60 Club" was started by the bank in late 1974. Overall the bank has a 30 percent share of the retail market, double the size of its nearest competitor. Because of the large, affluent market represented in Santa Barbara and the interest in trust services, the bank has more trust assets than it does banking assets. More than 7,000 members belong to the Club. The program is so well known in the community that very little advertising is required to enhance the program.

In-bank teller training is conducted the first week of every month. The sessions train new tellers on how to deal with the elderly. Emphasis is placed on how to treat them as potential "Our Gang" members. Among the topics covered are speaking more slowly so that customers understand, practicing communications techniques to make sure they understand what a teller is conveying and generally ways in which the bank employee must change in dealing with the differences between the younger and the older customer.

Retail banking personnel, particularly young tellers and personal bankers, need special training to understand the importance of senior customers, says Schneider.[8] They need assertiveness training because they are sometimes intimidated by the directness, experience and shopping knowledge of older customers.

According to him, some need to be taught to be sensitive to seniors' needs and not to be put off by their occasional slowness and talkativeness. Equally important, they need information about the competition so they can answer detailed questions seniors frequently raise.

In addition to training, well-written and produced in-bank communications can create awareness by all bank employees of the value and special handling that this market segment dictates. Sunwest Bank in Albuquerque produced a clever, visually appealing seven minute videotape for all bank employees. The tape used a Hollywood-in-the-twenties motif to introduce its packaged seniors account. Meridian Bank in Reading, Pennsylvania, conducted employee meetings with a 1960s flair, including the bank's top officers wearing high school letter sweaters. And, a band played '60s music for dancing after the formal program and dinner.

The Market's Concern Over Safety and Soundness

The issue of safety and soundness is a vital concern in the relationship with older customers, one which bank employees must be extremely sensitive to and must be prepared to deal with in an assuring way.[9] The greatest need of midlife and older customers is the assurance that their savings and investments are safe and secure in a financial services institution.

In the American Banker's 1987 Consumer Survey, customer confidence in the health and stability of the financial industry declined to its lowest level in the four years the newspaper has been polling customers. The news of loan defaults at banks, the economic slowdown in many parts of the country, and the concern over higher interest rates is keeping the older customer on edge.

Many of them remember a time when savings accounts in banks were not as safe as they are now. They remember "bank holidays" and closures and are deeply concerned about the economic soundness of their own bank....The October 19 stock market crash had a significant effect on older bank customers. They became frightened of the possibility of losing a large amount of hard-earned assets. Many of them left the stock and bond market for the safer insured savings.

Trust and confidence in the banking system motivates the older customer more than the younger one. They look to their banker to help explain the events in the financial services industry, especially those of a negative nature. Many a bank branch manager is asked to explain news articles about bank failures that customers read in the national and local press. One branch manager told me mature customers tear out articles in the newspaper, bring them to her and ask her to explain what is happening.

Physical Limitations

In an area where many employees have little appreciation or understanding, programs such as these are necessary to communicate the significant differences. Understanding the difference between an older customer and a younger one begins with understanding the process of aging.

The problem is that most financial services marketers know very little about the psychological and physical changes that occur within the post-50 market.[10] The majority of marketers and customer-contact personnel are usually much younger and, naturally, their perspective is one of a younger person. To overcome this age gap, a number of banks have instituted training programs to help customer-contact employees understand the physical and psychological needs of the market.

There is a marked difference between those over 65 and those under. The process of aging is a natural one that begins to impose limitations on sight, hearing, and muscle control. The quality of life for older individuals improves when stress arising from these limitations is reduced. Two of the most significant sources of stress are concerns over health and finances.

It is imperative for the financial services marketer targeting this market to realize that success rests with the bank's ability to reduce the level of stress for older customers. Understanding the physical differences that lead to stressful situations is at the core of the program.

Vision, hearing, touch sensitivity and muscle strength are the major areas in which the aging process produces physical change. Visual impairment in the U. S. ranks third on the list of chronic diseases restricting adult activity. In 1987, 62 percent of the U.S. population was wearing eyeglasses, a high number indeed.

Vision Problems with the Elderly

The physical ability to see and read is an integral part of the buying habits of the older consumer. More than any other segment, the older customer relies on and makes decisions most often based on materials provided by the product or service provider. While their need for reading ability is great, their ability to read is diminished.

Vision changes may occur any time during a normal person's life. They occur more frequently with advancing age. After age 50, the loss of "accommodation capacity of the normal eye," or clear vision over a range of distances, is close to 100 percent.

The older individual often has limited capacity to see objects that are near. Seeing depends on the size of the object, the distance the object is from the eye and the amount of light.

The effect can be startling. Simmons Market Research says its research shows that 60 percent of older consumers cannot read the size of type used on packages and labels. Increasing the size of type for promotional brochures directed to the older consumer by 50 percent is one way to aid the communication process.

A bank should use backlit in-bank displays with low contrast and low level lighting. Since older consumers also have difficulty adjusting to changing amounts of light, reduce the amount of glare in in-bank and external lighting displays. Avoid lighting in television commercials that frequently switches from bright to low intensity.

Another visual acuity problem for the older customer is distinguishing colors at the same level of intensity, especially on textured or glossy surfaces. Extremely light tones, dark shades and colors at the lower end of the spectrum like blues, greens and purples—are hard to distinguish.

As a general rule, increasing the level of background lighting and choosing strongly contrasting colors will improve communications with the older customer.

113

Hearing Deterioration

Deterioration in hearing occurs at about the same pace as deterioration in vision. It tends to stabilize during the early and middle years but increases in the later years. More people have difficulty hearing than seeing, and hearing problems occur more often in men than women.

Hearing problems result in misunderstanding or lack of comprehension. When there is little background noise or if the oral communication is presented clearly, the older customer has few problems. Loss of hearing tends to distort certain frequencies. As a result, turning up the volume on a hearing aid only increases the confusion.

Older persons have more hearing difficulty with certain consonants, especially with the letter S. Hearing problems are multiplied in settings with poor listening conditions.

Oral communication that is speeded up or interrupted for any reason adversely affects the mature person's ability to understand. Sound that bounces off a hard surface also becomes distorted. The bank that understands these problems may attempt to reduce the number of surfaces that cause reverberation, reducing or eliminating background noise through acoustical design, and training personnel to speak more slowly and distinctly—without appearing to patronize the older customer.

Tellers should write down account balances, interest rates or other pertinent information legibly—and give the piece of paper to the customer. They also need to count currency carefully and slowly, in plain view, so the customer is assured that the count is accurate.

Touch Sensitivity

The older person does not notice temperature changes as readily as a younger person. As a result, body-temperature mechanisms do not react as quickly. The older customer is more apt to complain of temperature extremes.

The temperature setting of branch locations will need to match those needs if the financial services marketer desires to keep stressful situations at a minimum. One approach may be to change the temperature setting at different times of the day. Retired, older customers tend to visit the branch during less crowded hours—9:30 to 11 a.m. and 2 to 4 p.m.

Regarding muscle strength: There is little reduction in an individual's physical strength until the person reaches 40, and minimal loss from then until age 60 or 70. After that, muscle loss is much more severe.

Strength loss is more prevalent in legs than in hands and arms. The fear of falling becomes a reality to many older persons as they enter their 70s. Each year, 30,000 people are disabled by falling. It also is the second leading cause of death by accident from ages 45 to 75 and the leading cause for those over 75 years of age. Falls are caused by the natural aging process of bones that are weakened, slower reactions, decreasing vision and hearing and other contributing factors—illness, medication and strength loss.

Bank's branches should be designed to include door handles, knobs and buttons that are easy to operate. Handrails on stairways should permit the individual to fully grasp the handle to allow the individual to use full strength. Many older people compensate for their lack of physical strength by using body weight to open heavy doors that open out.

The placement of furniture in the bank's customer traffic patterns is also critical, given the level of declining vision by older customers. Tile and linoleum floors, rugs or carpets need to be securely fastened. Non-skid wax should be used on bare floors.

ABA's "Older Bank Customers" Program

The American Bankers Association has developed a sensitivity program in conjunction with the American Association of Retired Persons to assist front-line personnel become aware of older person's characteristics and needs. The Program Kit includes a leader's guide for a three to six hour workshop, a 15-minute slide-tape or videotape presentation, and 20 copies of the Participant's Workbook and Manager's Brochure.

The day-long workshop is designed to help bank tellers, platform personnel, other customer contact staff and managers deal responsibly and productively with older customers. The workshop includes sessions on why the older population is an important market for banks; concerns about dealing with older customers; a picture of the lifestyles, health, income, and activities of older people; society's stereotyped views about aging that present barriers to dealing effectively with older customers; coping with physical problems; and techniques for transactions with older customers.

Our Recommendations

☐ Employee sensitivity training will only be a part of the bank's efforts if management calls for action in the targeting of a segmentation strategy toward the mature customer. If top management is not aware of the impact, it is marketing's responsibility to develop awareness within the bank.

☐ Employee sensitivity begins with a training plan. It should be a shared project between marketing and the training or human relations function.

☐ Many local agencies have professionals who are experts in gerontology, aging, healthcare and lifestyles of the older person. They usually are available to work with any groups interested in the older citizen. Use those resources to the fullest.

☐ Among the best resources for dealing with older people are older people themselves. Identify one or several individuals who can work with the bank in developing training programs. Often these individuals will work for small wages because of the limitations imposed on them by Social Security eligibility. They are at a stage in their life where they seek satisfying tasks like this.

☐ Evaluate a number of packaged programs such as the one available from the American Bankers Association. A purchased program saves the wear and tear of developing a training curriculum.

Notes
1. George Rieder, *Journal of Retail Banking,* 1984, P. 12.
2. Michael P. Sullivan, "Employees: Untapped Marketing Resource," *NABW Journal,* September/October, 1984, P. 4.
3. Data from First Union National Bank in 1985 when co-author Michael P. Sullivan was Director of Corporate Communications.
4. Jim Schneider, "Seniors—The Rising Stars of Relationship Banking," *Bank Marketing,* January, 1987, P. 43.
5. David Wolfe, "The Four Faces of the New Senior," *Marketing Communications,* March, 1988.
6. "Marketing Strategies," *Selling to Seniors,* October 1988,
7. Linda Ellis, "Thrifts Promote Good Health, Sensitivity; Seminars Tackle Special Problems of Senior Citizens," *American Banker,* July 3, 1987, P. 6.
8. Op. Cit., Schneider, P. 42.
9. Michael P. Sullivan, "Helping Older Customers Cope With Bank Mergers," *American Banker,* July 28, 1988, P. 4.
10. Charles D. Schewe, "Marketing to Our Aging Population: Responding to Physiological Changes," *Journal of Consumer Marketing,* Summer, 1988, P. 61.

Conclusion

This book was written to provide you with a basic understanding of the mature market and its importance, and to help you take advantage of it to improve your bank's bottom line. If there is one message that we could pass on it would be: Pursue the mature market.

Some marketing trends are here today and gone tomorrow. The mature market trend is not a fad—it is here to stay. As the baby boom starts turning 50, the mass market and the mature market will become one and the same.

As your bank begins to launch a special club or membership program to serve the growing dynamic mature market, or enhances an existing program, it is going to be very important to constantly monitor the results. A recent survey on the mature market conducted by a syndicated research firm reveals that older customers are very confused about financial service packages offered by most banks.

As more and more financial institutions launch programs targeting the mature customer the benefits and services will become difficult to distinguish, more clouded and confusing. There will be more clutter, more choices, and more competition, thus causing even more confusion to the customer making those choices. Your bank's mature market program will have to be unique and packaged differently from others in the same trading area.

Stay close to the mature market. It is important to get constant feedback and input from your current and potential customers. They are the best teachers. They can provide you with invaluable information that will help you develop meaningful packages of services that they will use.

The most important thing is to provide services to this market segment that have perceived value and benefit. Communicate the information in an easy-to-understand manner. Always emphasize the benefits. Be sure to differentiate your bank's program from all your competitors'.

What We See on the Horizon

The mature market is dynamic, diverse and complex, and it will become even more so. The buying behavior and savings habits of the mature market will change. For example, until now ATMs and electronic banking services have not been well received by mature customers. This will change as the gadget-driven, computer-literate baby boom generation ages and becomes the mature market.

At this point is it hard to predict if the aging baby boomer will be a funds user or a funds provider in the future, and it is important to watch for indications of how their banking needs are changing. Today, for example, there are signs that they are beginning to move away from heavy use of installment credit, which provides traditional fee income generated from credit cards.

Baby boomers have watched their parents retire, and in many instances are now guiding their parent's retirement. According to the Mature Market Institute, it is important to identify these new older-parent/child relationships and use this intergenerational marketing opportunity in developing your marketing strategies.

The mature market of tomorrow will continue to search for personal quality service from their primary financial institution.

Women will be an increasingly important market for financial institutions as today's working women age. Look for innovative ways to provide financial services to the mature woman, to help her build a financial nest egg as well as provide her with information on caregiving and financial planning.

Those who develop new products at your bank will have to start looking at new financial products and services that will generate fee income. Products like health insurance, savings programs, caregiver programs, reverse mortgages and new credit/debit card services will have to be developed for the mature market.

Mature customers will be loyal as long as your bank continues to provide financial services and products that help them ensure and maintain their lifestyle. You cannot afford to ignore the competition for this valued customer, and you will have to constantly bring new services, products and enhancements to your bank to keep them.

The mature market is here to stay. The bank that is here to stay is one that continues to be inventive, unique and creative in serving this dynamic, diverse market segment.

Appendix: Resources

Organizations

Council on Financial Competition
The Advisory Board Company
501 C Street, NE
Washington, DC 20002
Membership information: (202) 223-2932

Mature Market Institute
Box 6223
Washington, DC 20015
(202) 363-9644

The National Council on the Aging, Inc.
600 Maryland Avenue, SW
West Wing 100
Washington, DC 10024

American Society on Aging
833 Market Street, Suite 516
San Francisco, CA 94103

International Society of Pre-Retirement Planners
11312 Old Club Road
Rockville, MD 20852-4537

Bank Marketing Association
309 West Washington Street
Chicago, IL 60606
(312) 782-1442

Federal Government Agencies

U.S. Department of Health and Human Services
Office of Human Development Services
Federal Council on the Aging
HHS-N Bldg.
330 Independence Ave., SW
Washington, DC 20201(202) 245-0441
Charles J. Fahey, Chm.

Established under the authority of the Older Americans Comprehensive Service Amendments of 1973, P.L. 93-29, the Council is a Presidential advisory committee and assumed many of the duties of the Advisory Committee on Older Americans, which has been terminated.

The Council was created to advise the President, Secretary of Health and Human Services, Commissioner on Aging, and Congress on matters relating to the special needs of older Americans. It is composed of 15 members appointed by the President, with the approval of the Senate. Members are to be representative of older Americans, national organizations with an interest in aging, business, labor and the general public. At least five members shall themselves be older persons.

U.S. Department of Health and Human Services
Public Health Service
Alcohol, Drug Abuse and Mental Health Administration
National Institute of Mental Health
Special Mental Health Programs Division
Centers for Studies of Mental Health of the Aging
Parklawn Bldg.
5600 Fishers Lane
Rockville, MD 20857 (301) 443-1185
Dr. Gene D. Cohen, Chief

The major role of the Center is to stimulate, coordinate, and support research, training, and technical assistance efforts relating to aging and mental health. Program responsibilities include: 1) research support of studies which have a primary focus on the mental health and illness implications of the aging process and of old age; 2) research training through National Research Service Awards, including individual fellowships and institutional awards at the predoctoral and postdoctoral levels; 3) clinical/services manpower training grants that focus on training efforts designed to improve mental health and related services to the aging within the established mental health service delivery system; and 4) technical assistance and dissemination through consultation in order to develop and stimulate research and training applications focused on the mental health of aging persons.

U.S. Department of Agriculture
Agricultural Research Service
Human Nutrition Research Center on Aging
Tufts University
15 Kneeland St.
Boston, MA 02111 (617) 956-7571
Dr. Hamish N. Munro, Dir.

The Center plans and conducts research on nutrient needs of the elderly and the relation of dietary factors to the aging process. The program includes studies on; 1) nutritional needs for optimal health, function, and performance throughout the lifespan; 2) the physiological and biochemical factors associated with aging which influence dietary requirements; and 3) dietary factors which influence the aging process.

U.S. Department of Health and Human Services
Office of Human Development Services
Administration on Aging
HHS-N Bldg.
330 Independence Ave., SW
Washington, DC 20201 (202) 245-0827
M. Gene Handelsman, Actg. Commr.

The Administration on Aging (AOA) is the principal federal organization for identifying the needs, concerns, and interests of older persons and for carrying out the programs of the Older Americans Act. AOA is also the principal agency for promoting coordination of federal resources available to meet the needs of older persons.

Under Title III of the Older Americans Act of 1965, as amended (42 U.S.C. 3001 et seq.), AOA administers a program of formula grants to state agencies on aging to serve as advocates for the elderly and to assist in the establishment of comprehensive, coordinated service systems for older persons of the community level. State agencies designate and fund area agencies on aging, which serve as advocates for the elderly within their communities. In addition, area agencies plan and manage the delivery of a variety of social services and nutrition services which are authorized under Title III. AOA also can make direct grants to qualified Indian tribal organizations to support social and nutrition services for older Native Americans.

AOA awards grants for research, demonstrations, and manpower development projects. In addition, AOA operates the National Clearinghouse on Aging.

U.S. Department of Health and Human Services
Public Health Service
National Institutes of Health
National Institutes on Aging (NIA)
National Institutes of Health, Bldg. 31
9000 Rockville Pike
Bethesda, MD 20205(301) 496-1752
Dr. Robert N. Butler, Dir.

The Institute conducts and supports research on the biological, medical, psychological, and social aspects of aging through its intramural and extramural and collaborative research programs. Most of NIA's intramural (in-house) research is conducted at the Gerontology Research Center in Baltimore, MD. The Extramural and Collaborative Research Program (ECRP) supports studies on aging at universities, hospitals, medical centers, and nonprofit institutions throughout the U.S. Funds are made available for these studies through a variety of grant and contract mechanisms. (The Institute also supports the training of scientists for research careers in aging). Biological and medical research is supported on four levels: 1) molecular studies, which include research on the mechanisms of age-dependent changes in kidney function, muscle activity, heart function, and metabolism; 2) cellular and comparative physiology studies, including support of a cell-culture bank to establish, characterize, store, and distribute standard and genetically-marked cell lines for aging research (available to qualified investigators); 3) animal model investigations, including studies in immunology, nutrition, pharmacology, and endocrinology; and 4) investigations in man, including the Baltimore Longitudinal Study, as well as studies in immunology and endocrinology. (As part of its program involving animal model investigations, NIA's

Extramural and Collaborative Research Program supports development of colonies of aged rodents which will be made available to scientists conducting gerontology studies.) A fifth level of research supported by NIA involves behavioral and social studies on the psychological and social aspects of aging.

U.S. Department of Health and Human Services
Public Health Service
National Institutes of Health
National Institute on Aging
Gerontology Research Center
Baltimore City Hospitals
4940 Eastern Ave.
Baltimore, MD 21224 (301) 396-9421
Dr. Richard C. Greulich, Dir.

The Center's laboratories conduct quantitative and qualitative research on the process of aging in animals, including man. Principal areas of study are: 1) clinical physiology, which includes sections on metabolism, human performance, endocrinology, cardiovascular studies, and clinical immunology; 2) behavioral sciences, including psychophysiology, learning and problem solving, and stress and coping; 3) molecular biology and cellular physiology, with sections on intermediary metabolism, inorganic biochemistry, macromolecules, cellular aging, and genetics; and 4) neurosciences.

U.S. Department of Health and Human Services
Social Security Administration
6401 Security Blvd.
Baltimore, MD 21235 (301) 594-1988
John A. Suahn, Commr.

The Social Security Administration administers a national program of contributory social insurance which pays benefits when earnings stop or are reduced because a worker retires, dies or becomes disabled. Disability insurance (SSDI) provides a partial replacement of monthly earnings to disabled persons who meet work requirements for eligibility. After 24 months of receiving benefits under SSDI, persons automatically qualify for hospital and medical insurance under Medicare. (Persons of any age who need kidney dialysis or kidney transplant for permanent kidney failure also may be eligible for Medicare. Medicare protection for these people starts with the third month after they begin maintenance dialysis. Under certain conditions, protection can begin earlier).

Clearinghouses and Information Centers

U.S. Department of Health and Human Services
Office of Human Development Services
Administration on Aging
National Clearinghouse on Aging
HHS-N Bldg.
330 Independence Ave., SW
Washington, DC 20201 (202) 245-0188
Donald Smith, Dir.

The National Clearinghouse on Aging collects, analyzes, and disseminates information on the problems and circumstances of the aging population and its impact on the social system. The wide range of subject areas covered by the Clearinghouse includes nutrition, housing, health, employment, supportive social services, legislation, and training for professionals who work with aging persons. The Clearinghouse responds to inquiries on all aspects of aging by sending copies of Clearinghouse fact sheets, bibliographies, and other publications. When appropriate, inquirers are referred to other information centers or to direct service providers, including the state agencies on aging, which offer a variety of services to older Americans. Fact sheets are available on federal programs which assist the elderly, employment and volunteer opportunities for older persons, educational possibilities for older persons, retirement housing, crime prevention, transportation, recreation, audio-visual materials sponsored by AOA, and other topics. A brochure entitled "To Find the Way" outlines major sources of assistance for older Americans. SCAN, the Service Center for Aging Information, is the component of the Clearinghouse which sponsors a bibliographic information retrieval system under contract. The system consists of a Central Control Facility for processing documents and three Resource Centers for collecting, indexing, and abstracting documents.

University of Southern California
Ethel Percy Andrus Gerontology Center
Andrus Gerontological Information
University Park
Los Angeles, CA 90007 (213) 743-5990
Jean E. Mueller, Chief Librarian

The Andrus Gerontological Information Center (AGIC) identifies, collects, abstracts, indexes, and disseminates bibliographic materials in the field of aging, with emphasis on social and behavioral aspects. In support of its work, AGIC produces the machine-readable AGEX (Andrus Gerontological Exchange) data base, which contains bibliographic citations to nonjournal literature held in its library. This input literature includes books, monographs, government documents, doctoral dissertations, research reports, model project reports, bibliographies, and selected secondary sources. The Center provides computerized searches from AGEX and all relevant commercially available data bases. It also issues bibliographies and provides document delivery services for materials published by the Gerontology Center.

123

State Government Agencies

Alabama Commission on Aging
2853 Fairlane Drive
Montgomery, AL 36130 (205) 832-6640

Alaska Department of Health and Social Services
Office on Aging
Pouch H-01C
Juneau, AK 99811 (907) 465-3253

Arizona Department of Economic Security—Division of Aging, Family
and Children's Services
1717 W. Jefferson Street
Phoenix, AZ 85005 (602) 255-3596

Arkansas Department of Human Services—Office on Aging and
Adult Services
Donaghey Bldg.
7th and Main Streets
Little Rock, AR 72201 (501) 371-2571

California Health and Welfare Agency—Department of Aging
918 J Street
Sacramento, CA 95814 (916) 322-5290

Colorado Department of Social Services—Division of Services for
the Aging
1575 Sherman St.
Denver, CO 80203 (303) 839-2586

Connecticut Department on Aging
Washington St.
Hartford, CT 06115 (203) 566-3238

Delaware Department of Health and Social Services—Division of Aging
Delaware State Hospital
New Castle, DE 19720 (302) 421-6791

District of Columbia Office of the Mayor—Office of Aging
1012 14th St., NW
Washington, DC 20005 (202) 724-5622

Florida Department of Health and Rehabilitation Services—Program
Office of Aging and Adult Services
1323 Winewood Blvd.
Tallahassee, FL 32301 (904) 488-2650

Georgia Department of Human Resources—Office of Aging
47 Trinity Ave., SW
Atlanta, GA 30334 (404) 894-4440

Hawaii Executive Office on Aging
1149 Bethel St.
Honolulu, HI 96813 (808) 548-2593

Idaho Office on Aging
700 W. State
Boise, ID 83720 (208) 334-3833

Illinois Department on Aging
421 E. Capitol Avenue
Springfield, IL 62706 (217) 785-2870

Indiana Commission on Aging and Aged
Graphic Arts Bldg.
215 N. Senate Ave.
Indianapolis, IN 46202 (317) 232-1194

Iowa Commission on Aging
Jewett Bldg.
415 10th Street
Des Moines, IA 50319 (515) 281-5187

Kansas Department of Aging
610 W. 10th Street
Topeka, KS 66612 (913) 296-4986

Kentucky Department of Human Resources—Bureau for Social
    Services—Office of Aging Services
Human Resources Bldg.
275 E. Main St.
Frankfort, KY 40601 (502) 564-6930

Louisiana Office of Human Development—Aging Section
PO Box 44367, Capitol Station
Baton Rouge, LA 70804 (504) 342-2297

Maine Department of Human Services—Bureau of Maine's Elderly
State House
Augusta, ME 04333 (207) 289-2561

Maryland Office on Aging
State Office Bldg.
301 W. Preston Street
Baltimore, MD 21201 (301) 383-6393

Maryland State Department of Health and Mental Hygiene-Services to
    the Aging
201 W. Preston Street
Baltimore, MD 21201 (301) 383-2723

Massachusetts Department of Elder Affairs
110 Tremont St.
Boston, MA 02108 (617) 727-7750

Michigan Department of Management and Budget—Office of Services to
    the Aging
300 E. Michigan
Lansing, MI 48909 (517) 373-8230

Minnesota State Department of Public Welfare—Aging Program Division
658 Cedar St.
St. Paul, MN 55155 (612) 296-6193

Mississippi Council on Aging
802 N. State
Jackson, MS 39201 (601) 354-6590

Missouri Department of Social Services—Division of Aging
Broadway State Office Bldg.
Jefferson City, MO 65102 (314) 751-3082

Montana Department of Social and Rehabilitation Services—
    Aging Services Bureau
PO Box 4210
Helena, MT 59601 (406) 449-5650

Nebraska Commission on Aging
State House Station 95044
Lincoln, NE 68509 (402) 471-2306

Nevada Department of Human Resources—Division for Aging Services
505 E. King St.
Carson City, NV 89710 (702) 885-4210

New Hampshire State Council on Aging
14 Depot Street
Concord, NH 03301 (603) 271-2751

New Jersey Department of Community Affairs—Division on Aging
363 W. State Street
Trenton, NJ 08625 (609) 292-4833

New Mexico State Agency on Aging
Chamisa Hill Building
440 St. Michael's Drive
Santa Fe, NM 87503 (505) 827-2802

New York State Office for the Aging
Agency Bldg. 2
Empire State Plaza
Albany, NY 12223 (518) 474-4425

North Carolina Department of Human Resources—Division of Aging
325 N. Salisbury St.
Raleigh, NC 27611 (919) 733-3983

North Dakota Social Services Board of North Dakota—Aging Services
State Capitol Bldg.
Bismarck, ND 58505 (701) 224-2577

Ohio Commission on Aging
50 W. Broad St.
Columbus, OH 43215 (614) 466-5500

Oklahoma Department of Human Services—Special Unit on Aging
PO Box 25352
Oklahoma City, OK 73125 (405) 521-3531

Oregon Human Resources Department—Office of Elderly Affairs
722 Commercial St., SE
Salem, OR 97310 (503) 378-4728

Pennsylvania Department of Aging
Finance Bldg., Rm. 404
Harrisburg, PA 17120 (717) 783-1550

Rhode Island Department of Elderly Affairs
79 Washington St.
Providence, RI 02903 (401) 277-2861

South Carolina State Commission on Aging
915 Main St.
Columbia, SC 29201 (803) 958-2576

South Dakota Department of Social Services—Office of Adult Services
   and Aging
Richard F. Kneip Bldg.
Pierre, SD 57501 (605) 773-3656

Tennessee State Commission on Aging
535 Church St.
Nashville, TN 37219 (615) 741-2056

Texas Governor's Committee on Aging
Executive Office Bldg.
211 E. 7th St.
Austin, TX 78711 (512) 475-2717

Utah State Department of Social Services—Division of Aging
150 W. North Temple
Salt Lake City, UT 84103 (801) 533-6422

Vermont Agency of Human Services—Office on Aging
State Office Bldg.
Waterbury, VT 05676 (802) 241-2400

Central Vermont Council on Aging
18 S. Main St.
Barre, VT 05641 (802) 479-0531

Virgina Office of Human Resources—Office on Aging
830 E. Main St.
Richmond, VA 23219 (804) 786-7894

Washington Department of Social and Health Services—
   Bureau of Aging
OB44
Olympia, WA 98504 (206) 753-2502

West Virginia Commission on Aging
State Capitol
Charleston, WV 25305 (304) 348-3317

Wisconsin Department of Health and Social Services—Bureau of Aging
One W. Wilson St.
Madison, WI 53702 (608) 266-2536

Wyoming Department of Health and Social Services—Office on Aging
Hathaway Bldg.
Cheyenne, WY 82002 (307) 777-7986

Puerto Rico Department of Social Services—Division of Geriatrics
PO Box 11390
Santurce, PR 00910 (809) 724-7400

Publications

Publications FOR the Mature Market

Efforts to reach the mature market should include media that specifically cover this group. The shift in population and recognition of this demographic segment have led to the launches of many senior publications and syndicated columns. Many of the leading U.S. dailies have assigned reporters to cover this group. Likewise, numerous general interest, financial, lifestyle and medical publications and broadcast programs regularly devote space and air time to issues facing seniors.

When the marketing plan calls for advertising or public relations efforts, the following media should be considered. Please note that personnel changes at these columns and publications are frequent. It's best to check by telephone for current responsibilities.

Magazines

Mr. Bard Lindeman, Editor
50 Plus Magazine
850 Third Avenue
New York, NY 10022
(212) 715-2767

Ms. Carol Osmon, Editor
California Senior Citizen
4805 Alta Canyada Road
La Canada, CA 91011
(818) 683-1344

Mr. Don McLellan, Editor
Elder Statesman
1201 W. Pender Street #301
Vancouver, B.C. V6E 2V2, Canada
(604) 683-1344

Ms. Carol Brenner Hittner, Editor
Golden Years
233 E. New Haven Avenue
PO Box 537
Melbourne, FL 32901
(305) 725-4888

Mr. George Bush, Editor
Grandparents
1716 Locust St.
Des Moines, IA 50336
(515) 284-3000

Ms. Jeannette Hofmann, Editor
Leisure Life
PO Box 872
San Jacinto, CA 92383
(714) 654-9759

Dr. Larry Tout, Editor
Mature Health
PO Box 1675
Midland, MI 48640
(517) 687-5555

Ms. Elizabeth Brewster, Managing Editor
Mature Outlook
3701 W. Lake
PO Box 1205
Glenview, IL 60025
(312) 291-4739

Ms. Susan J. Sands, Editor
The Mature Traveler
PO Box 141
Pitman, NJ 08071

Mr. Dennis Sumrow, Editor/Publisher
Maturity Monthly
Maturity Monthly Fresno
8046 Calif City Blvd./#A
PO Box 2074
California City, CA 93505

Mr. Ian Ledgerwood, Editor
Modern Maturity
3200 E. Carson Street
Lakewood, CA 90712
(213) 496-2277

Ms. Shirley Copithorne, Editor
New England Senior Citizen
Senior American News
470 Boston Post Road
Weston, MA 02193
(617) 899-2702

Mr. Dennis Cerrotti, Editor
The Older American
110 Arlington Street
Boston, MA 02116
(617) 426-0805

Mr. Stan Allen, Editor
Retirement Life
1533 New Hampshire Avenue NW
Washington, DC 20036
(202) 232-4000

Ms. Georgia Voils, Editor
Senior Citizen Newspaper
PO Box 666
Godfrey, IL 62035
(616) 466-4916

Mr. Don Lowry, Editor
Senior Life
PO Box 640
Failbrook, CA 92028
(619) 738-3722

Mr. Fred Birkman, Editor
Senior Spectrum Monthly
941 Willora/#C
Stockton, CA 95207
(209) 474-8887

Ms. Roxane Provence, Editor
Senior Times
2207 S. 48th St./#A
Tempe, AZ 85282
(602) 438-1566

Ms. Betty Marie, Editor
The Senior Tribune
1509 Johnson Ferry Rd./#B-20
Marietta, GA 30062
(404) 971-0197

Ms. Laura Impastato, Executive Editor
Senior World of California
1000 Pioneer Way
PO Box 1565
El Cajon, CA 92022
(619) 442-4404

Mr. Jay A. Binkly, Editor
Silver Circle
1001 Commerice Drive
Irwindale, CA 91706

Syndicated Columnists

Dr. Muriel Oberleder
"Avoid the Aging Trap"
Singer Communications
3164 W. Tyler Avenue
Anaheim, CA 92801
(714) 527-5650

Mr. Sid Ascher
"The Best Years"
214 Boston Avenue
Mays Landing, NJ 08330
(609) 927-1842

Mr. Guy Bartin
"Easy Does It"
PO Box 1662
Pittsburgh, PA 15230
(412) 391-4361

Mr. Bard Lindeman
"In Your Prime"
50 Plus
850 Third Avenue
New York, NY 10022
(212) 715-2784

Mr. Leonard J. Hansen
"Mainly for Seniors"
Copley News
PO Box 190
350 Camino De La Reina
San Diego, CA 92108
(619) 293-1818

Mr. Larry Miller
"Larry Miller"
22600 Dolorosa Street
Woodland Hills, CA 91367
(213) 462-6371

Ms. Elyse Saland
"On Aging"
UCS Department of Medicine
10833 Le Comte Avenue
Los Angeles, CA 90024
(213) 825-8255

Mr. Carl Riblet Jr.
"Past 65"
PO Box 40757
Tuscon, AZ 85717
(602) 881-2931

Ms. Jolayne Far
"Prime Times"
Miller Services Ltd.
180 Bloor St. W.
Toronto, ON 5F2V6
(416) 925-4323

Mr. Harold Blumenfeld
"Retirement"
137 Golden Isles Drive
Hallandale, FL 33009
(305) 454-0066

Mr. Harry Rosenthal
"Harry Rosenthal"
Associated Press
2021 K St., NW/6th Floor
Washington, DC 20006
(202) 828-6457

Dr. H. Frank MacInnes
"Senior Clinic"
HFM Literary
PO Box 307
Edmonton, Alberta T5J2J7
(403) 973-2361

Mr. Kent Collins
"Senior Forum"
L.A. Times Syndicate
Times-Mirror Square
Los Angeles, CA 90053
(213) 972-5000

Ms. Matilda Charles
"Senior Service Line"
301 E. 73rd St.
New York, NY 10021
(212) 772-1420

Mr. Rowland B. Smith
"Something to Think About"
Sand Dollar Bldg./Suite 907
Shell Point Village
Fort Meyers, FL 33908
(813) 466-4425

Ms. Cheryl Jensen
"Taking Care"
12700 Lake Avenue/#2203
Lakewood, OH 44107
(216) 226-8990

Mr. John W. Newton
"Threescore and More"
251 Atlantic Avenue
Marblehead, MA 01945
(617) 631-6287

Mr. Jack H. Smith
"Time of Your Life"
11085 Tom Shaw Drive
El Paso, TX 79936
(915) 593-2412

Ms. Patricia Galbraeith
"Yes, You Can"
PO Box 368
Weatherford, TX 76086
(817) 594-4415

Editor
"Your Social Security"
Copley News
350 Camino de la Reina
PO Box 190
San Diego, CA 92108
(619) 293-1818

Publications ABOUT the Mature Market

American Demographics Magazine
108 North Cayuga Street
Ithaca, NY 14851
(800) 273-6343

Aging Network News
PO Box 1223
McLean, VA 22101
(monthly tabloid)

Selling to Seniors, A Monthly Report on Marketing
8555 16th Street, Suite 100
Silver Spring, MD 20910
(301) 588-6380

Mature Market Report
801 East Campbell, Suite 110
Richardson, TX 75081
(monthly newsletter)

Modern Maturity
1909 K Street, NW
Washington, DC 10049
(bi-monthly publication of AARP
requires $5.00 membership in AARP)

Maturity Market Perspectives Newsletter
P.O. Box 6472
Annapolis, MD 21401
(monthly newsletter—(301) 268-0730)

Mature Outlook
6001 North Clark Street
Chicago, IL 10660
(bi-monthly publication
Membership in the Sears family of companies is required)

New Choices
Retirement Living Publishing Company
PO Box 1945
Marion, Ohio 43305-1945
(Owned by Reader's Digest)

Lear's
"For the Woman Who Wasn't Born Yesterday"
505 Park Avenue
New York, NY 10023
(Bi-monthly consumer publication)

Golden Years
Senior Services Group
233 East New Haven Avenue
Melbourne, FL 32901
(monthly publication)

Senior Market Report
244 W. 54th Street, Suite 706
New York, NY 10019
(monthly newsletter—1-800-331-1931)

135

Bibliography

R.J. Balkite, "Improving Ads to the 50 and Over Customer." *Inside Print,* October, 1987.

Laurie Carney, "Strategic Offensive at Bank IV Local Battle in 'Senior War.'" *Bank Marketing,* September, 1987.

"Chem's Pitching Pensions to Well-To-Do Self-Employed." *Crain's New York Business,* January 16, 1989.

"Closing the Gap." *AARP News Bulletin,* November, 1987.

Catherine A. Cole and Michael J. Houston, "Encoding and Media Effects on Consumer Learning Deficiencies in the Elderly." *Journal of Marketing Research,* February, 1987.

Robert F. Collins, Jr., "Senior Programs—A 'Golden' Opportunity to Provide Bank-Centered Lifestyles." *Bank Marketing,* March, 1988.

The Conference Board, *Midlife and Beyond: The $800 Billion Over-Fifty Market,* 1985. Prepared by the Consumer Research Center in a study sponsored by CBS/Broadcast Group, CBS Magazine and CBS Economics.

Barry I. Deutch, "Effective Retail Promotion Assures Sources of Funding." *American Banker,* March 23, 1989.

Ken Dychtwald and Joe Flower, *Age Wave: The Challenges and Opportunities of an Aging America.* Los Angeles: Jeremy Tarcher, 1989.

Linda Ellis, "Thrifts Promote Good Health, Sensitivity; Seminars Tackle Special Problems of Senior Citizens." *American Banker,* July 3, 1987.

Robert Essers and Don Christenson, "Market Segmentation: Effective Design and Use in Financial Service Institutions." *Journal of Retail Banking,* Winter, 1987.

"Financial Clout of Seniors Drawing Increased Attention." *Marketing Update,* Bank Marketing Association, September, 1987.

"Going for the Gray." *ABA Banking Journal,* April, 1989.

James O. Gollub, *Business Opportunities among the Aging Population.* SRI International Business Intelligence Program, Summer, 1984.

Alan J. Greco, "Linking Dimensions of the Elderly Market to Market Planning." *Journal of Consumer Marketing,* Spring, 1987.

Helen Harris and Vicki Thomas, "Tune into the Mature Market." Unpublished manuscript.

"How Americans View Their Financial Service." Consumer Survey, *American Banker,* Special Report, 1987.

William Lazer and Eric H. Shaw, "How Older Americans Spend Their Money." *American Demographics,* July, 1987.

James R. Lumpkin and Troy Festervand, "Purchase Information Sources of the Elderly." *Journal of Advertising Research,* December, 1987-January, 1988.

"Marketing Strategies." *Selling to Seniors,* October, 1988.

The Daniel Yankelovich Group, Inc., *The Mature Americans—A Study of Today's Men and Women 50 Years and Older.* For *Modern Maturity,* Fall, 1987.

George Miaoulis, Ph.D. and Phillip Cooper, Ph.D., "The Grey Market Lights Up the Satisfaction Syndrome." *Marketing Communications,* March, 1987.

George Miaoulis, Ph.D., and Phillip Cooper, Ph.D., "The Satisfaction Syndrome." *Marketing Communications,* March, 1987.

Eileen Norris, "Radio listens closely to the Mature Market." *Advertising Age,* October 19, 1987.

Jeff Ostroff, "An Aging Market: How Business Can Prosper." *American Demographics,* May, 1989.

Thomas J. Rinella, "Packaging Services to Create Added Value." *Bank Marketing,* November, 1988.

Jay Rosenstein, "Bank Branches in Retirement Villages Tap Lucrative Market With Small Outlay." *American Banker,* July 28, 1988.

Randall Rothenberg, "Campaigns That Turn Off Older Americans." *The New York Times,* May 30, 1988.

Georgia E. Scheppner, "Target the Older Market." *Real Estate Today,* April, 1987. Jim Schneider, "Seniors—The Rising Stars of Relationship Banking." *Bank Marketing,* January, 1987.

Charles D. Schewe, "Marketing to Our Aging Population: Responding to Physiological Changes." *Journal of Consumer Marketing,* Summer, 1988.

Frank L. Schick, ed., *The Statistical Handbook on Aging Americans.* Phoenix: Oryx Press, 1986.

Jeffry Scott, "The 55-Plus Crowd Is Still Kicking—and Buying." *Adweek,* October 31, 1988.

Senior Recreational Doubles. USTA Publications, USTA Seniors Tennis, Princeton, NJ.

S. Sherman, "Reported Reason Retired Workers Left Their Last Job: Findings From the New Beneficiary Survey." *Social Security Bulletin,* March, 1985.

Gerald Sword, "Beliefs and Behavior." *Shea's Quarterly,* July-September, 1988.

"Special Report—A Survey of Senior Newsletter Publications." *Mature Market Report,* 1988.

Hilary Stout, "Free At Last—To Spend More Money." *The New York Times,* September 11, 1988.

Michael P. Sullivan, *A Bankers Guide to the Mature Market.* Easton, PA: Christmas Club, A Corporation, August, 1988.

Michael P. Sullivan, "Employees: Untapped Marketing Resource." *NABW Journal,* September/October, 1984.

Michael P. Sullivan, "Helping Older Customers Cope with Bank Mergers." *American Banker,* July 28, 1988.

Chester A. Swanson, "Marketing and Reaching the Ageless Market." *RAB Sound Management,* December, 1987.

U.S. Senate Special Committee on Aging. *Aging in America: Trends and Projections, 1987-88 Edition.* Prepared with the American Association of Retired Persons, the Federal Council on Aging and the U.S. Administration on Aging. Washington: U.S. Department of Health and Human Services.

Anthony C. Ursic, Michael L. Ursic, Virginia L. Ursic, "A Longitudinal Study of the Use of the Elderly in Magazine Advertising." *Journal of Consumer Research,* June, 1986.

Sandra van der Merwe, "GRAMPIES: A New Breed of Consumers Comes of Age." *Business Horizons,* November-December, 1987.

"Women in the Workplace." *Working Age,* AARP, January/February, 1988.

David Wolfe, "The Ageless Market." *American Demographics,* July, 1987.

David Wolfe, "The Four Faces of the New Senior." *Marketing Communications,* March, 1988.

The Who and How-to of the Nifty 50 + Market. New York: Grey Advertising.

The Authors

Vicki Thomas is president of Thomas & Partners Co., Inc., a four-year-old full-service promotional agency that develops marketing strategies, provides promotional avenues, develops unique senior bank programs, and conducts focus groups to assist clients in effectively targeting the customer 50 and over.

Thomas plans, designs and implements mature market programs for banks, credit unions, savings & loans, and brokerage firms. She is a certified pre-retirement consultant and trainer and a nationally recognized authority on the mature market segment. Thomas is co-producing a five-part retirement related series on housing, health, finance, insurance and career and educational opportunities in retirement for Connecticut Public Television. She is also producing a "Dancin' Grannie" exercise video and health fairs featuring the Grannies.

Prior to forming Thomas & Partners, Thomas worked for the American Broadcasting Company in the Sales Promotion and Affiliate Services Division in New York City and was Vice President of Marketing and Advertising for Credit Union National Association, headquartered in Madison, Wisconsin.

Thomas is a member of the International Association of Pre-retirement Planners, American Society on Aging, the Mature Market Institute and is on the Development Advisory Board for Connecticut Public Television.

Michael P. Sullivan heads a marketing and communications consulting firm specializing in developing bank programs for the mature market customer.

Sullivan has devoted nearly 20 years to the financial services industry as a banker, banking association executive and industry consultant. He is widely known throughout the industry for his writing and speaking. He is a regular columnist in the *American Banker* daily newspaper, writing in the Marketing Management column since 1980, and has written two books on marketing for the American Bankers Association.

Previously, as vice president of corporate communications for First Union National Bank, he was responsible for public relations, employee communications and investor relations for the 24th largest U.S. bank. He has also been editor of *Bank Marketing* magazine and head of communications for the Bank Marketing Association.

Sullivan has a journalism degree from the University of Detroit and an M.B.A. from Wayne State University in Detroit. He is chairman of the Financial Service Section of the Public Relations Society of America, where he is accredited.